GIFTS
FROM
HEAVEN

GIFTS
FROM
HEAVEN

True Stories of
Miraculous Answers to Prayer

COMPILED BY
JAMES STUART BELL

BETHANYHOUSE
a division of Baker Publishing Group
Minneapolis, Minnesota

Published by Bethany House Publishers
11400 Hampshire Avenue South
Bloomington, Minnesota 55438
www.bethanyhouse.com

Bethany House Publishers is a division of
Baker Publishing Group, Grand Rapids, Michigan

Printed in the United States of America

Library of Congress Cataloging-in-Publication Data
Names: Bell, James S., compiler.
Title: Gifts from heaven : true stories of miraculous answers to prayer / compiled by James Stuart Bell.
Description: Minneapolis, Minnesota : Bethany House, 2017.
Identifiers: LCCN 2016036511 | ISBN 9780764217869 (trade paper : alk. paper)
Subjects: LCSH: Prayer—Christianity. | Miracles—Anecdotes.
Classification: LCC BV220 .G54 2017 | DDC 248.3/2—dc23
LC record available at https://lccn.loc.gov/2016036511

The following are true stories, but some details and names have been changed in order to protect privacy.

Editorial services provided by Jeanette Gardner Littleton Publication Services

Cover design by LOOK Design Studio

17 18 19 20 21 22 23   7 6 5 4 3 2 1

To Margaret:

How beautiful, then, the marriage of two Christians, two who are one in hope, one in desire, one in the way of life they follow, one in the religion they practice. They are as brother and sister, both servants of the same Master. Nothing divides them, either in flesh or in spirit. They are, in very truth, two in one flesh; and where there is but one flesh there is also but one spirit. They pray together, they worship together, they fast together; instructing one another, encouraging one another, strengthening one another.

—Tertullian (to his wife)

The best and sweetest flowers of paradise God gives to His people when they are upon their knees. Prayer is the gate of heaven.

—Thomas Brooks

Contents

Contents

Contents

Contents

Acknowledgments

With much gratitude for a superb team—among others, David Horton, Andy McGuire, Ellen Chalifoux, Julie Smith, and Carissa Maki.

Introduction

Do you ever have doubts that God answers or even really hears some of your prayers? The truth is that God responds to any and every prayer of the heart. Oftentimes, however, we may not be aware of how He responds to our praises, our requests, or our frustrations. We only know by faith that He is actively and lovingly responding and working through those prayers, as He tells us in Scripture.

Sometimes we have doubts because we don't physically see results from our prayers that we would like to see in our lives. Some of us wonder if we have prayed hard enough or sincerely enough, or if there were obstacles in our lives that prevented His positive answers. Yet most of us can recall certain times in our walk with God when He came through for us with flying colors, when we just knew it could only be His doing. He is the God of the impossible and the miraculous, and there are times when His power is so evident that all we can do is marvel and break out in praise to Him.

This volume is a collection of stories of believers who needed God to come through in a big way and He did just that, sometimes in a much bigger way than they expected. Everything we receive from God is truly a gift, whether it relates to our health, our talents, our families, or the provision of some particular need. There are other gifts of His grace that can only be described as supernatural. They go beyond the norm in our lives, displaying His power and distinct presence, His divine intervention when we're desperate. These answers are truly "gifts from heaven" that stem from His abounding love and generosity.

I hope this volume will encourage you, the reader, to persist in seeking all the precious gifts God has to offer. My prayer is that knowing how His everlasting love has blessed others, you will seek Him to fulfill your dreams and supply your needs. But above all, may you see Him manifested clearly as the Great Gift Giver, and cherish the Giver more than His gifts. For as it says in James 1:17, "Every good gift and every perfect gift is from above, coming down from the Father of lights with whom there is no variation or shadow due to change" (ESV).

God desires to give you good and perfect gifts from heaven, as these contributors herein attest. I hope today that you can see the radiance of His glory, where no wavering exists, because He is for you—yesterday, today, and forever.

James Stuart Bell

God's Intrusion

BRENDA DILLON

W hether it was shock, relief, or unexplainable awe that put me in a state of speechlessness, I'll never know. I do know, however, that while my tongue was silent, my mind and heart were having a very serious emotional conversation with the Lord Jesus.

Seven years had passed since I had been diagnosed with an abnormal tricuspid heart valve. The doctor explained that a normal tricuspid valve was round and had three flaps, making it look like a peace sign. Mine, however, was oval with two flaps, making it look like an egg with a smile.

At the time, I thought, *No big deal—it works.* But the doctor told me I needed to have it checked every year—which, of course, went directly to the bottom of my to-do list.

Moving ahead seven years, I went to see my family doctor for a checkup, and he asked how the bicuspid was doing. When I told him I'd never had it checked, he immediately sent me to the other side of the building to see the heart doctor—who immediately sent me downstairs to radiology for an ultrasound.

It was a little unnerving when a technician asked to witness my test because she had never seen such an abnormality in real life.

Why not—bring in the whole crew!

I had second thoughts about that as more technicians began to hover over me, and the test seemed to go on and on. I remembered the earlier procedure only taking ten to fifteen minutes. I lay there watching the hands on the wall clock tick off the minutes, while the confused technicians took turns looking at the ultrasound screen connected to my heart and checking it against my previous films.

I'm sure they must have seen a slight jolt on the monitor as I remembered the doctor holding up my films, pointing to the "smiling egg," and explaining to me that the flaps on a bicuspid valve were more apt to wear out than the flaps on a normal tricuspid valve.

I began to think about all the time I had spent hiking the peaks and canyons of our friend's ranch in the Big Horn Mountains. With every remembered step I thought, *I was wearing out my flappers . . . I was wearing out my flappers!*

Being one week away from my next trip to the ranch, a foreboding melancholy came over me. There would be no hiking this fall—maybe never again. As I lay there, feeling darker and darker, I heard a technician use the word *suspicious,* and in my mind, that sealed my fate. Heart surgery was surely going to keep me from my annual adventure—perhaps permanently.

No, Lord, please! You know how much I love the mountains—you put that love in me. You and I have had wonderful times together scaling the peaks and creeping through the canyons. I feel so close to you when I stand on those rocky heights. Besides, I already have my plane ticket purchased. You know that I dearly love you and that my faith in you has a strong foundation. I believe that your heart always desires the best for me. So if this is what you want to use in my life for continued growth and blessing, I surrender it to you. But please let me go to the mountains one last time.

I was finally told they were finished, but that I needed to see the doctor before I left. I said a quick prayer and stepped into his office.

He stood there with all my films hanging on the examination wall. He slowly pointed out the "smiling egg" of seven years ago—I remembered it well. Then, with a shaking hand, he pointed to the perfectly shaped "peace sign" they had recorded that day.

He must have said a dozen times, "I can't understand this! I've never seen anything like this."

I asked if I had somehow grown another "flap," and with irritation in his voice he said, "No! You're born with these things, you don't grow them."

If I hadn't seen the tests with my own eyes, I might have thought the films had gotten mixed up. But those were all my films—with my name, my birthdate, and the calendar date of each test printed on the corners.

There was only one answer to the mystery. For whatever reason, God had chosen to turn my bicuspid heart valve into a perfectly working tricuspid valve.

The doctor said, "You don't have to come back," and I couldn't get out of the building fast enough.

When I reached my car, the tears cut loose. Not just tears of joy over the new miracle valve, but tears that came from the recognition that my God had chosen to lovingly intervene in my life in such a way that I couldn't doubt the source. One week later, I was worshiping God on top of a red-rock ridge in the Big Horn Mountains of Wyoming.

This miraculous intrusion by my Father God was a faith-building tool that He used to strengthen my spiritual foundation and increase my ability to trust Him in any situation.

Eleven years have passed since God performed a miraculous surgery on a heart that has been Christ's home for many years. His welcomed intrusions and constant presence have continued to build my faith and make Him very dear to me.

James 4:2 says we have not because we ask not. Matthew 13:57–58 says Jesus did few miracles in His hometown because of their unbelief. My desire is to never limit God by not asking or by not believing He can do something if He so chooses.

Each time He and I go hiking in the mountains, we have long discussions about how He renovated His home—both spiritually and physically.

Face-to-Face With Jesus

DELORES E. TOPLIFF

I f I only had a few days' rest, I could get back on top of things," my husband's youngest sister, Valerie, said. Her husband, Richard, was out west on a business trip. She sighed. "As darling as our kids are, it's hard taking care of two little girls and a five-month-old boy by myself."

"At least Doug's a good-natured baby."

"Yes, he is." She squeezed him.

I studied his sturdy limbs, his adorable wispy curls above dark brown eyes. "When does Richard get back?"

"Monday night."

"Doug drinks from a bottle now, doesn't he?"

"That's right. I couldn't manage otherwise." Valerie sank against the soft sofa cushions, looking exhausted.

I sat beside her. "Here, let me hold him." As I lifted him, he snuggled without fussing. This was Friday evening. I didn't have classes again until Monday. My husband, Jerome, and

I exchanged glances. My eyes asked the question. His eyes answered.

"Valerie, my homework's caught up—no classes until Monday. If you think . . ." I swallowed. "I mean, if you'd be willing to trust me, we'd love to have him for the weekend."

When I patted Doug's cheek, he cooed.

Relief flooded her face. "Are you serious?"

"Yes," I said, with more confidence than I may have felt. "I've watched you care for him. I helped lots with my younger brother when he was little and he survived. Is there anything special I'd need to know?"

"Not really—not that I can think of. Phone if anything comes up."

Jerome chucked Doug under his chin; he grinned.

I shifted the baby's weight in my arms, and his smile grew. "Look, he understands. He's okay with us." My confidence grew.

"It looks that way. Wow. If you're sure, that would be amazing." Valerie gathered a few items in a diaper bag. "He's a good little guy. Here's lots of diapers, one prepared bottle, and plenty of formula."

She slid the diaper bag strap over my shoulder and kissed Doug's sweet forehead. "I love you, Dougie." He waved and cooed.

"Thanks so much," she said with a sigh. "A few days of rest will make me as good as new."

"It'll be fun. We're glad to help." It was after 10 p.m. on a warm summer night in Richmond Hill, north of Toronto. We drove south on Highway 404, slowing to the posted 45 miles per hour as we entered the residential area, though few houses were visible yet. The highway was well lit with little traffic. Road conditions were perfect.

Doug slept, wrapped in a blanket across my lap in those days before infant car seats. When he stirred minutes later, I felt impressed to give him his bottle immediately, before he woke up. Shifting him into the well-anchored football position, I placed the bottle in his mouth. I'd no sooner gripped him securely, when something very large, loud, and fast crashed into us from behind.

Brakes squealed and torn metal screamed as our car crumpled and the violent impact propelled us forward. The steering wheel held Jerome upright, but his driver's door was torn off the frame and left behind on the highway.

Everything happened so fast. The magnetic flashlight on the front of our dash broke free and circled in the air. Though baby Doug's bottle was torn from my hand and joined the spinning flashlight, he stayed secure. Whatever hit us had such force it snapped the substantial solid steel rod across our car's front seat that released it to a complete fold-down bed. I was thrown into the back seat, still clutching baby Doug tight.

Until then, I hadn't believed people who said their whole lives flashed before them when they faced possible death, but mine did now.

As Doug and I flew to the back seat, with our car careening crazily forward, out of control, I asked the Lord, *Is this it? Are you taking us home?*

Badly shaken, with objects flying everywhere, my husband managed to steer the car to the shoulder, finally stopping.

I scrambled out with Doug. That's when I heard and saw Jesus—face-to-face.

"What did He look like?" people ask.

"Like you would expect," I answer. He appears in ways familiar to us, I think, so that we'll recognize Him.

21

Back in Sunday school days, I'd always loved the Sallman's Head of Christ portrait, so that's how Jesus appeared to me. Calm. Solid. Smiling. Real. With honey-brown hair curling to His shoulders, warm brown eyes, and wearing a long, simple home-spun robe. He stood so near in the twilight, I could have reached out and touched Him. But it was enough to bask in His presence.

Clutching Doug close, I felt cocooned in peace. Jesus was there with us, only three or four feet away.

"Your time is not yet," He said, love and peace emanating from His warm gaze. *"I have more for you to do."* I heard His soft, reassuring voice. Comforting.

I felt safe, surrounded by great peace. I knew no serious harm could reach us.

I turned to Jerome. "The Lord is here. Do you see Him?"

He answered, "No, but I believe you. I feel the peace."

Several things happened very fast. A car driving the opposite direction squealed to a stop as the driver ran to us, carrying a black leather bag. "I'm a news photographer with the *Toronto Globe and Mail.*" He hauled out a huge camera and started clicking away. "I saw the whole thing, so I'm taking these pictures and can be your witness. The driver didn't hit his brakes at all. It's almost like he hit you on purpose."

The police came. The seventeen-year-old driver who'd crashed his father's heavy car into us was going nearly 80 in a 45-mph zone. He didn't have his headlights on and didn't engage his brakes.

The young man was unhurt, since his car was so large and heavy. But he tested positive for drugs, lost his license, and faced serious charges.

Our car was totaled and missing a door, but we could drive home very slowly. Severe whiplash troubled me for years, but eventually subsided. Best of all, clutched safe and secure in my tight football hold, since I'd given baby Doug his bottle as soon as he stirred, he suffered no harm at all. Several doctors said if the steel rod controlling the release of our car's front seat hadn't broken completely, throwing Doug and me into the back seat, my neck would have snapped, paralyzing or killing me.

What I recall most about that unforgettable night is Jesus' loving presence reassuring me that He had a plan and purpose for our lives through every circumstance. Although we've faced tests since then, He's always kept His word.

The Voice of My Maker

CASSIE HARRIS

Accord to the neurologists, I am an unsolvable mystery. My apparently incurable epilepsy is a prime example of why even the wisest doctors say they only *practice* medicine.

Neurologists loved gazing at the statistics of my young life, seeming to hope their next perusal would give a cure. The doctors never received their wish. It seemed as if all they truly knew were the two most basic things about my case: my name and the disease that rocked my body without mercy.

At sixteen years old, I had undergone two brain surgeries and tried hundreds of medications to find relief from the disease that had become my identity. Regardless of the doctors' relentless efforts, I experienced nearly thirty seizures a day with no light at the end of the tunnel. I was in survival mode.

I lived in a paradox. Understandably, I hated the seizures that took my mind and body captive. With my type of epilepsy, if anyone tried to help me during a seizure, they ran the risk of causing permanent brain damage.

I hated the loneliness I was forced to endure because of the disease. However, as a born-again Christian, I found that within the seizures I was granted an unfathomable audience with my Lord and Savior, Jesus Christ. My loved ones couldn't touch or talk to me without causing me harm, but Jesus could.

As anyone who bears a chronic disorder will tell you, trusting God's love gets more difficult the longer you wait on answers. I knew God loved me. I knew the Scripture verses to prove that God is who He says He is and He will do what He says He will do. I had the head knowledge.

But the head knowledge often broke my heart when I faced baffled confusion. *God is good? If God is good, why won't He heal me?*

If I wasn't faced with questions of God's goodness, His mere existence was often questioned when people looked at my life.

I begged God to reveal His love for me in undeniable ways. I had accepted the reality that I may not be healed this side of heaven. Whether healing would be a part of my story or not, I was desperate for proof that I was not the only human being God's mercy hadn't reach. I longed to have a story of miraculous healing to tell my children and grandchildren for years to come. What would be better than telling a story of a faithful God who took a child at death's door and restored her to full health?

Over time, God revealed the beauty of *not* healing me. In firm yet merciful ways, He showed me how my life spoke of His miraculous grace and mercy *because* He didn't heal me. I was made to glorify Him; who was I to tell Him He'd messed up so badly He couldn't use my diseased body? Who was I to declare that God's deity was not strong enough to supersede my disabilities, to work within them, not in spite of them?

"You may not understand how I'm using your trials," He seemed to whisper. *"Start looking for ways I intervene to spare your life. Look for the small miracles, child. There are so many things I have given you to shout my love for you from the rooftops. The problem is you're too busy looking for what I haven't given you. Look for my glory in my interventions and the ways I have stayed by your side. You will find me there."*

One day stands out in my mind when I remember Jesus' miraculous intervention in my life. On average, my seizures would last only a few minutes, though each second felt like a torturous eternity. We had been told that seizures more than ten minutes could cause permanent brain damage.

On this particular day, the seizure had lasted almost seven minutes. My mother stood near the bed I was lying on, trying to be supportive in a silent, inactive way.

Epileptics are taught how to test their own brain function during a seizure. It is not uncommon to hear an epileptic come out of a seizure muttering simple facts such as his or her name, birthday, and the country's current president. During bouts of mental lucidity, I formed the one-syllable question I could manage with my disobedient tongue.

"Name?" I couldn't comprehend what such a word meant, let alone the answer. I simply clung to the fact that somewhere in my mind, an answer to that question would gain my mind's freedom.

"Name?!" I shouted louder, pounding the bed with my jolting fists. Only silence met my inquiry. Panic filled every fiber of my being.

"Jesus! Jesus! *Name?*" I screamed desperately.

Somewhere in the dark, tortured recesses of my mind, I heard a man's voice singing, *"I am your maker. I know your name."*

As the seizure continued, hope rushed to the forefront of my mind. I knew that voice. It was the voice of my Maker.

"Child! My name. My name is Child of God," I forced out between the violent jolts of my muscles. "Child of God! I'm a child of God!"

Instantly, the seizure stopped. I was free!

Quietly, I joined the voice of my maker God in the familiar song He was singing over me. "He knows my name. . . ."

I made eye contact with my mother. Tears sprang to our eyes as we looked at a clock. The seizure had lasted nine minutes and 45 seconds. God had relieved my body of its temporary torture with only seconds to spare.

During that seizure, I grasped an even deeper understanding of God's miraculous love. His greatest desire for us is that we learn to lean into the power and security we are given as His children. Every other blessing pales in comparison. Because of His miraculous love, I am not a mere survivor of epilepsy. He intervened in my life, and because of my faith in Him, He made me a victor over death.

He Opened My Eyes

Jeff Adams

*B*am!
   My eye seemed to explode into waves of pain as I crumpled to the floor.

I'd only turned my head for a moment to look at my racquetball opponent, Phil. But meanwhile, he had hit the ball, and it slammed into my left eye, breaking my glasses, cutting my eyebrow, and knocking me off my feet with the unexpected force.

The owner of the club looked at my injury. "You should get a couple of stitches," he advised. Reluctantly, I went to the ER, where a doctor assessed, "Two stitches." Someone came in with a sewing kit.

Afterward, with the outside of my eye clean and ready for a bandage, I asked, "When will I be able to see again?"

The physician assistant froze. "What do you mean?"

"I can't see."

"Open your eye." I did. No one had asked me to do that previously. They didn't think to because they could see the obvious problem. I thought somehow blood from the cut had covered the outside of my eyeball, making it impossible for me to see. *If you just wash it out, I'll be fine.*

"Stay right here," the PA said. "Don't go anywhere. Don't move."

"Okay."

The ophthalmologist joined the Worry Club that the PA chartered on my behalf. My cheery demeanor could easily be mistaken as a mask for panic. But I was not in shock because I simply didn't know the seriousness of my injury. Dr. Shaw did.

"What do you see?"

Not much. "I can tell if the lights are on or off."

"Open your eye, slowly." Presumably she gave that direction to avoid further trauma to my eye. The light I detected from the ceiling suddenly became gray. I asked what she did. "I blocked the light. Do you know how I did that?"

I had no clue. "Did you stand in front of me?" She said nothing. "Did you turn off the light?"

"Neither. I moved my hand in front of your face."

I had no sense of how near or far her hand had been in proximity to my face. I couldn't tell how big her hand was or how many fingers she held up or whether her hand was balled up in a fist or her palm was open. I couldn't see anything.

"Look up. No, no. Don't move your head. Just your eyes."

No change.

"Look down."

Still the same.

29

"Left." I complied. "Now right." I shook my head.

She already knew. "You have a hyphema." I must have looked puzzled. "The blood isn't on the outside. It's inside."

That doesn't sound good.

Had the accident happened two weeks earlier, I don't know what would have been done for me. Fortunately, Dr. Shaw had moved to our little town, giving us something we didn't have before—an ophthalmologist who could diagnose a hyphema.

"A hyphema is blood inside the anterior chamber of the eye, the space between the cornea and the iris. The blood is covering everything—the iris and the pupil. The white part of your eye is all red. That blood in the eye chamber is blocking your vision completely."

Such an injury is typically painful. My eye ached, but the pain didn't leave me in agony. I remained calm throughout her examination. That may have also contributed to her decision to keep me overnight for observation.

Before an aid took me upstairs, Dr. Shaw gave the good news and the bad news.

"There's nothing I can do. There's no surgery or medication."

I signed some forms and climbed off the table into the waiting wheelchair. "We'll keep you sitting up tonight and I'll see you in the morning."

You'll see me, but will I see you? I thought.

"The blood may drain a bit, but you still won't be able to see." Then she added, "You'll be legally blind."

Yeah, but I still have my right eye. I'll manage.

"There's a 70 percent chance you'll develop glaucoma in the other eye. If the blood in the left eye doesn't drain, over time the intraocular pressure could cause glaucoma."

I learned later that the injury to my left eye might produce trauma in my good eye that would result in irreversible optic nerve damage in both eyes.

She might as well have told me, "Get a dog and learn braille. You'll need both."

I thought that, but quickly dismissed it. "We prayed. God will come through."

Anyone could summarize the extent of my friend Phil's and my knowledge of God in less than one minute: "Two Testaments. Four gospels. Some incredible stories. An apple. A flood. A guy swallowed by a whale. Two tablets with Ten Commandments that we seemed unable to keep. Jesus. Born to Mary, a virgin. Crucified. Dead. Buried. Rose from the dead on a Sunday. Our sins were forgiven."

We were too young in the faith not to believe God still works miracles. And I couldn't comprehend how much I needed one. So we just believed. Along with others.

Our pastor, Allen, and assistant pastor, Carl, came to the hospital. They prayed. They asked God to do the impossible. I believed anything was possible.

Although I'd grown up in church, I'd only come to faith in Jesus within the past year. Ordained as a deacon in a mainline denominational church, I heard the gospel. I could recite the Apostle's Creed, but I had no relationship with Jesus. Instead, I tried to keep God's rules, because if I didn't, well, there'd be hell to pay.

I did bad things for so many years, and I rarely did what I knew I should do. But no matter how hard I tried, nothing ever changed. I was in an impossible situation, and I needed a miracle.

That miracle came when I surrendered my life to God.

I can't fix me. I'm too broken, I'd prayed. I'd asked God to help me because I couldn't help myself.

Now, unable to see, I knew I once again faced an impossible situation. But that night one thing was different—I had hope. "Faith shows the reality of what we hope for; it is the evidence of things we cannot see" (Hebrews 11:1 NLT).

I'll just trust God. There's nothing else I can do.

The elders in our church anointed me with oil. They prayed. Nothing changed.

Upstairs, alone in a brightly lit room, I could see with only one eye. I sat propped up in the bed. Rather than being depressed or worrying about what my life would be like as a thirty-one-year-old blind man, I peeked. I lifted the bandage that covered my left eye. Nothing. *Not yet.*

The Bible talks about the gift of faith. It's something extra, something above and beyond what all of us are given—a measure of faith. God doesn't give it because we want it; He bestows it because we need it, when we need it.

Midnight had passed, and I couldn't sleep. I was too excited. I expected to see. That's why I kept peeking from beneath the bandage. That's why I describe the initial answer to my prayer as a gift of faith. Years of diligent study did not produce that faith. Faithful attendance and service didn't generate it. Sacrificial giving didn't purchase it. Years of prayer didn't build up my faith to supernatural proportions. I believed. Like a child, I trusted my Dad. I knew He loved me. I believed He wanted me to see again. I didn't doubt. Not because I possessed faith greater than other people, but because I believed just enough.

Moreover, it wasn't what I believed but who I trusted that made the difference. I believed God would keep His promise. "Your Father knows the things you need before you ask him"

(Matthew 6:8 NCV)! I peeked. Still no change. Nevertheless, I'd ask, just to make sure. "You don't get what you want because you don't ask God for it" (James 4:2 PHILLIPS).

God, please. I lifted the bandage. It was still night. "Everything good comes from God" (James 1:17 ERV). I believed God would do what I asked Him to do because He loved me, not because I'd been a good boy.

I peeked a few more times. Not because I wanted proof. I had that. But because I'd been assured. I prayed once more before I drifted off into a blissful sleep. *Thank you.*

What might have happened if I hadn't prayed? What if others hadn't prayed? My pastors? The church elders? It's not easy to speculate about what doesn't happen because a miracle does. All I know is that I was blind and now I see. I went to bed unable to distinguish anything except whether a light was on, and that only so long as no one played a trick on me and blocked the light from my eyes.

The next morning, Dr. Shaw's exam room was dark. My wife handed me my prescription sunglasses. Dr. Shaw lifted the bandage away from my injured eye. She covered my good eye.

"Take your time and try to focus. Tell me if you can see anything."

I smiled. I saw my wife, Rosemary.

"Can you read anything on the chart?"

I read the jumbled letters, line after line, until I got to DEFPO-TEC, and kept reading. 20/15. 20/12. 20/10. There was nothing else to read. But the doctor had more to say.

I'd read the chart. God answered my prayer and the prayers of others. He gave me a miracle. But she wasn't convinced.

"Just remember, there's still a 70 percent chance of glaucoma in the other eye."

"Doctor, with all due respect," and I meant that, "Jesus didn't heal me now so I could get glaucoma later."

A subsequent exam, and others in the following years, confirmed God's goodness. It's been more than thirty-three years since that accident. There's no sign of any problem. In fact, we eventually learned why my eyesight actually improved.

Examined a week later for new glasses—because things didn't look right wearing my sunglasses—an optometrist listened to my story and confirmed my better eyesight. The force of the racquetball flattened my cornea, in much the way that Lasik surgery improves vision.

Curious why God stopped at 20/10, I prayed again. *You know I've hated wearing glasses since I was in grade school. Why didn't you fix my eyes so I don't have to wear glasses at all?* I waited a moment, then felt His whisper.

"You'd forget."

I understood. I remembered how Jacob limped after he wrestled with God. I doubt he forgot. I never have. Every time I clean my glasses, I remember that I was blind, but now I see.

The Mysterious Comforter

JOSHUA F. YOUNCE

I was driving south on Highway 23 in rural eastern Kentucky on August 19, 1999. I had driven that highway a thousand times to and from school, to football practice, and to court my fiancée. Our homes were about twenty minutes apart, and this would be one of the last times I would make this drive to pick her up while she was still using her maiden name—we were to be married in two days.

My fiancée and I had made the trip from the west suburbs of Chicago back home to Greenup, Kentucky, to be married in the church where she had grown up. A typical traditional wedding. Nothing fancy, nothing extraordinary, just a young man and woman ready to start their lives together.

I had met Cheri seven years before. She had attended a high school just fifteen minutes from mine, and we met at a combined high school function. I remember the first time I saw her—big brown eyes, dark hair, and a smile that lit up the room. She bubbled with personality and chatted with everyone. I, on the other hand, was "Mr. Cool Jock."

I was ready to enter my second year of chiropractic school in the fall. We had planned the wedding to coincide with one of my semester breaks. Cheri had just started a new job.

On the Thursday morning before our Saturday wedding we were scheduled to meet with the minister and to pick up the marriage license at the courthouse. I was staying with my parents, and that morning I was driving my brother's '88 Nissan pickup truck to her parents' house. Nervous, excited, happy—I was experiencing all the emotions a man goes through days before his wedding.

When I turned onto the highway, I saw maybe two or three cars on the road and a tractor pulling a hay baler—a common sight in rural Kentucky. As I approached the tractor driving 60 miles per hour, I looked over my left shoulder to see if I could move to the left passing lane. As I turned back to look in front of me, I saw a giant green wall.

I slammed on the brakes with the baler just fifteen feet in front of me. I smashed into it with a force that should have thrown me over the hills surrounding the highway.

No seat belt, no airbag, a tin-can truck, 60 miles per hour, and a baler that weighed at least 5,000 pounds. I honestly don't know how I survived.

I pulled myself up from the seat of the truck, and looked in the mirror. My face was vibrating, my body was numb, and blood covered me and the truck cab. I glanced around and no one was in sight.

I dropped back down to the seat of the truck.

"*Get up,*" a voice commanded. I wasn't sure whether it was in my head or coming from outside the truck, but I couldn't ignore it. I couldn't open the door, so I had to climb out the driver's window.

Stepping to the ground, I realized I couldn't put weight on my right leg, so I crawled to the side of the road, away from the smashed truck.

The tractor pulling the hay baler was 500 yards up the road; the driver apparently had not realized what happened. Then I saw that the baler had broken loose from the tractor. That's why it collided with me so quickly.

I started to cry. My face was shaking and my body hurt all over.

As anyone who has been hit in the face can tell you, the first thing you check is to see if any teeth are loose. No teeth were missing, but I was able to pull my left facial bone away from the rest of my skull. Then I started crying even more. I was to be married in two days and was badly hurt, and I was alone.

"*You're going to be all right,*" a man's voice spoke into in my left ear.

"*You're a tough football player. I know you. You're Josh, right?*" I continued to hear this voice in my left ear as an arm draped over my shoulder. "*Yeah, I know you. You'll be just fine. Say, what are you doing back here? I thought you lived in Chicago now.*"

I continued to stare straight ahead and answered, "I am getting married in two days."

"*Well, that's great. Congratulations!*"

Still not looking directly at him, I could see him out of my peripheral vision. He was a medium-height, husky guy, African-American, which was strange, because most folks around my hometown were white. He seemed to know me, but I never asked his name.

"Say, what are you doing in Chicago?" he asked. I told him I was in chiropractic school, studying to be a doctor. He laughed and said he was going to need me one day when I graduated, but I was going to have to open an office back in Kentucky.

He was on one knee beside me hugging me, comforting me, talking to me.

"You're going to be just fine. Help is coming. I'm going to stay right here with you until they get here. Say, you still playing football?"

I laughed, and so did he. "You've taken bigger hits in football than this one."

Right then I heard another voice: "Hey, hey, are you okay?" a woman spoke into my right ear. I turned to look at her and saw that it was a local woman I knew named Tammy.

"The ambulance is coming," she said.

I could hear the sirens now. I told her I was hurt pretty bad and thought I'd broken my face and right leg.

The ambulance took me to the nearest hospital about thirty minutes away. I was rushed into the emergency room to a team of physicians surrounding my bed. I felt like I was on the TV show *ER*, except I couldn't change the channel. They stabilized me and moved me quickly to a room.

Soon my fiancée, Cheri, my brother, and our parents were all surrounding me in the ER. They knew I was badly hurt. Tammy, the woman at my side when the ambulance came, had come to the hospital to see how I was.

"What happened, Tammy?" I asked. She said she didn't see the accident. She'd come upon the site probably ten minutes after it happened. I told her and everyone in the room, "Ask the guy who was there when you came."

"Honey, I was the first one there," she said. "There was nobody else there when I came."

"No, no, the black guy, who was sitting beside me on the ground. He was to my left talking to me. He had his arm around me. He must have seen everything," I said.

"Josh, you were sitting on the side of the road by yourself when I got there," Tammy assured me.

"He was there!" I insisted.

Two days passed in the hospital, and I was hooked up to a morphine drip, with ice bags on my face and leg, and still days away from the needed surgeries. With all that loomed ahead of us—a continued hospital stay, surgery, healing, school, Cheri's job, we decided not to delay the wedding. We married on the day we had planned, Saturday, August 21, 1999.

We crowded twenty or so family and friends into that little hospital room, including the minister, who happened to be my Little League coach and a family friend. Cheri's best friend and maid of honor sang "Valentine" as Cheri and I sat on the hospital bed together. There was not a dry eye in the room. We said our marriage vows and kissed.

After a few minutes passed, everyone left the room. I told Cheri I was so sorry for what had happened. She looked up at me with those big brown eyes—into my swollen, bruised face—and said she loved me and we would get through this.

Then she closed her eyes and prayed, *"God, we know you are still on the throne. I lift up Josh to you because you are the great physician. You are the Almighty God who holds us in your hands. Bring us safely through this and heal Josh's wounds, since we know you are the only one that is able. In Jesus' name. Amen."*

The chances were great that I could have died in that accident. God saved me for Cheri, and He was there with me, comforting me the whole time on the side of the road with His angel of mercy. Cheri knew it too and gave me another kiss. That's when you know you've got a great God and a great woman. Thank God He loves me that much.

The Healer
She Could Only Imagine

CHARLES EARL HARREL

The sun filtered through the alder trees on the hillside, causing our drenched lawn to glisten in the morning light. Saturated from an overnight storm, the ground still held small puddles.

We often had rain in Westport, Oregon. Sometimes, it seemed like the towns along the lower Columbia River basin experienced only two kinds of weather: wet and wetter. The night before had been one of the wetter ones. I decided to take advantage of the clear, dry conditions before the next storm moved in. My first project: trim back the wild blackberry forest that had spread out in every direction, crowding out the church's gravel parking lot.

After cutting blackberry vines for almost an hour, I heard the parsonage phone ring. I sprinted to the house, but by the time I got inside, the ringing had stopped. Out of breath, I paused a few minutes to see if my voicemail had recorded a message. The message indicator remained off.

"Hmmm, I wonder who was calling this early." I sat at the kitchen counter, poured another cup of coffee, and waited to see if the phone would ring again. It did. The person on the other end told me her name was Marilyn.

A physician from a nearby hospital had suggested that Marilyn talk with a minister or personal counselor. She had tried calling several churches listed in the Clatskanie Yellow Pages, but no one answered their phones or returned her messages. Frustrated, she decided to run some errands in town, fill her gas tank, and pick up a prescription at Hi-School Pharmacy.

She told me she had arrived at the drugstore a few minutes after it opened. Fortunately, only a few shoppers were milling about. As the pharmacist filled her order, she had waited silently, her eyes fixed on the floor. Attempting to make conversation, Becky, the pharmacy technician, inquired, "So, how are we doing today?"

Marilyn had broken down in tears, telling Becky about her lousy Monday morning and being unable to find a minister to consult with. Becky suggested she try the Westport Assembly of God Church and gave her my home phone number.

My conversation with Marilyn was brief. She wanted to see me, the sooner the better. She would give me the reason in person.

The next morning, Tuesday, at ten o'clock, I met with her in the church office. Her story broke my heart. Marilyn's mother had been in a coma at Columbia Memorial Hospital in Astoria, Oregon, for weeks. Vital organs were shutting down. Feeding tubes and a ventilator were keeping her alive. The attending physician had told Marilyn he and the hospital staff could do nothing more. He recommended removing the life support and allowing her mother to pass on.

Marilyn told me she had never been a religious person. In fact, she wasn't sure if God even existed. However, to please the concerned hospital doctor, she agreed to consult with a minister before making any final decision concerning her mother.

As Marilyn talked, tears ran down her cheeks. She looked emotionally worn out. She did not want to lose her mother, but didn't know how she could let her continue in a hopeless state.

"I only wish I had a little more time with Mom," she sighed.

I assumed Marilyn would ask me to go with her to the hospital, but she just wanted prayer to cope with her loss. Apparently, she had already made her decision based on the doctor's recommendation.

I didn't inquire about her mother's life story or ask for details about her illness. It didn't seem appropriate, considering the situation. I wept in my heart for her. Although I felt inadequate, I prayed for her to have strength and direction, and then added, "If a miracle is still possible, please give Marilyn her mother back." I ended with a quiet "Amen."

She only smiled a sad smile.

She arranged with the attending physician to disconnect her mom's life support on Thursday. Marilyn called me before leaving for the hospital to see if I could pray with her one more time. I asked her if she wanted me to accompany her, but she replied, "No, Reverend, this is something I have to do on my own."

So I offered another prayer, similar to the first, but this time Marilyn said "Amen" with me. She promised to call me back when it was over.

I waited for hours, but never heard back. Worry inundated my thoughts. I wondered if something had happened to Marilyn. Knowing how distraught she felt, the thought of her committing suicide crossed my mind. I started looking up the phone number for the hospital, when the phone rang. In haste, I almost dropped the receiver.

"Hello, Marilyn, is that you?"

I think she said *yes*, but someone nearby was talking with her, too, so I hesitated. After waiting a few more seconds, I continued with my rehearsed reply, "Marilyn, I am so sorry for your . . ." She cut me off mid-sentence.

"Reverend, you'll never guess what happened when they unplugged the life support equipment. My mom sat up in bed, looked around the room, and said, 'What the . . . !' I've been talking with Mom nonstop for two hours now. The staff already gave her some liquids and she's been eating gelatin and sipping chicken broth. She used the restroom, took a few steps around the hall, and now she's sitting in a chair. This is so wonderful! Her doctor thinks she can go home in a few days, after they figure out what happened. But I know what happened. It was a miracle, and the nursing staff believes it was a miracle, too. I am so happy! God is real after all. I have to go now. Just wanted to say thank you."

Overwhelmed, I thanked her for calling back and said something trivial like "You're welcome." However, I really don't think my efforts had anything to do with the outcome. Rather, it was a daughter's belief in a God she didn't know or understand, yet hoped would answer prayer and perform a miracle. All Marilyn desired was a little more time with her mother. In the end, God gave her more than she ever imagined.

I may not understand everything about divine intervention, miracles, or answered prayer. However, I have come to realize one thing: When we place our hope in God, the direst circumstances can become a springboard for the miraculous.

According to the apostle Paul, "[God] is able to do immeasurably more than all we ask or imagine, according to his power that is at work within us" (Ephesians 3:20).

Sometimes a simple *Amen* in faith is all that's needed.

The Angel Holdup

SUSAN ALLEN PANZICA

T hose stairs. They worry me. I pray every day for your
family on those stairs."

My husband's "crazy Aunt Anna" was always pray-
ing for something. For her, prayer was like breathing. She never
stopped until the day she died. She prayed for requests from local
churches and over prayer lists from televangelists. She prayed for
parking spaces, doctors' visits, and grocery orders. She prayed
herself up and down the few steps in her small apartment.

Aunt Anna was our family's rock of faith. A widow with
no children, she cared for her nieces and nephews, grandnieces
and grandnephews, as if they were her own. When my children
faced a pending test, audition, or big game, they'd ask Aunt
Anna to pray for them, believing that she had a direct line to
heaven. Of course, they knew that they could pray, too, but to
them, Aunt Anna's prayers seemed more powerful.

In her younger years, she visited people in need of prayer. My husband was often sick as a child, and Aunt Anna came to his bedside and prayed for him. Years later, as she became more housebound, she increased her prayer time. Her kitchen table served as prayer headquarters, strewn with handwritten prayers, journals, Bibles, devotional books, and prayer requests—lots and lots of prayer requests.

And for some reason, Aunt Anna always reminded us that she prayed for safety on our basement staircase.

What was it about those stairs that scared her? With her one withered hand and two arthritic knees, Aunt Anna had three good reasons to fear them. But we didn't. We climbed up and down those stairs each time we left and returned home. The handrail on the left side did seem a bit awkward when descending. Could that be it? Or was it the hard cement beneath the unpadded indoor/outdoor carpeting? Whatever it was, we didn't give the stairs a second thought.

Maybe we should have.

My four-year-old daughter's constant companion was her adorable talking doll, Katie. Lauren carried Katie everywhere she went, which was no small feat as the doll was half Lauren's height. Lauren was a petite, quiet little girl with a mass of brown curls. Katie was a huge blond doll that could robotically speak volumes.

One ordinary day, with our gathered belongings, we headed toward the stairs to the garage. My toddler son, A.J., rested heavily on my hip. Lauren carried Katie as she opened the basement door and started down the stairs.

What happened next took only a microsecond, yet it seemed to happen in slow motion. With the Katie doll in her left arm, Lauren stepped off the landing and made it to the second step before catapulting into the air. Her sneaker's thick rubber sole stuck on the carpet pile, propelling her headfirst down the hard flight of stairs. She rolled head over heels, gathering speed like a snowball in an avalanche.

Behind her, I was powerless to stop the unfolding nightmare as I envisioned my broken and bleeding little girl crumpled on the cement floor.

With teary eyes and pounding heart, I couldn't believe what I saw next. To this day, it seems like a film that's missing footage—as if several frames were lost on the cutting-room floor.

One second I saw Lauren flying. The next, I saw her twisted body at my feet lying diagonally on the stairs as if an angel had caught her in midair and gently laid her there. The rubber bottoms of her shoes faced up at me, her head a few steps down. The giant doll remained curled inside her left arm as her right hand somehow seized the railing on her left side.

Despite Lauren's wide-eyed terror, she didn't cry. She just waited calmly for me to gather her into my arms. As she nestled into my lap, her right hand—the one that held the banister—was balled in a fist. Prying her fingers open I found a huge wad of contraband gummy-worm candies nesting inside. Unbelievable! It was impossible for her tiny fist to have grasped the railing without dropping the candies.

I knew I had just witnessed an angelic intervention.

Matthew 18:10 says of little ones, "Their angels in heaven continually see the face of My Father who is in heaven" (NASB). The psalmist wrote, "He will order His angels to protect you wherever you go. They will hold you up with their hands so you won't even hurt your foot on a stone" (Psalm 91:11–12 NLT).

I believe God directly answered Aunt Anna's prayers. Surely He sent an invisible angel to keep Lauren from tumbling further down the stairs.

That day changed our attitude toward prayer, toward the presence of angels, and toward Aunt Anna. She was so faithful, so *sure* God heard her prayers—for big things and little things.

Taking our cue from Aunt Anna, my family and I now share *all* our concerns in prayer, not just the "major" ones. After all, the Bible says to "Give *all* your worries and cares to God, for He cares about you" (1 Peter 5:7 NLT, emphasis added). I now know He cares so much He even sends angels in times of need.

When she heard about God's answer to her prayer, Aunt Anna simply nodded knowingly, as she lived with the expectation that God not only heard her prayers but was a trustworthy steward of those prayers, answering them in His perfect method and timing. And through her prayers and faithful devotion, my family's faith in God grew—which I think was an answer to Aunt Anna's greatest prayer.

An Angel Named Grace

◆━━━━━━◆

BILL SHANE, AS TOLD TO DONNA LEE (SHANE) LOOMIS

*B*eep! *Whoosh! Hummm.*
    I wanted to silence the monitors over my head. But if the noise ceased, would I stop breathing? Would this troublesome heart stop beating? Would my fragile lungs stop taking in good air and releasing the bad?

What if they did? This body no longer does what I want it to do.

The hospital was quiet—as quiet as a hospital gets. The door to my room was open, and I could hear the call bells from the other rooms. The chatter and laughter from the nurses' station seemed incessant.

God, what do you want from me? What am I supposed to do with this tired body? I don't even have the strength to pound a nail let alone build a house, a cabinet, a dollhouse, or cradle!

*Picking up one of my grandchildren is more than I can handle.
God, what kind of life is this?*

*I love my family. Betty is the best wife a man could ask for,
and the girls and their families . . . I know they need me and
love me. But they are all taking care of me instead of my taking
care of them. I don't want to miss watching the grandkids grow
up. I don't want to leave Betty alone, and what about my girls?*

The battle raged in my mind. The ache in my back matched
my pounding head. I wanted nothing more than to sleep, and
yet sleep wouldn't come.

We'd made one more trip to the emergency room. I now
had a stent in my chest to protect my lungs and a pacemaker
to protect this troublesome heart.

Worries, fear, and discouragement were my constant companions. It appeared they'd be my only companions during
this long, long night. At the nurse's insistence, Betty, the girls,
and their families had all gone home. Supposedly rest was
the best thing for me. Didn't the nurses know my family was
what helped me hold on when this tired body was telling me
to just let go?

I knew from past experiences that the staff tried not to disturb
patients during the night. They depended on all those monitors
to alert them to anything wrong. The loneliness overwhelmed
me, though, and increased the fear. I didn't want to be alone.
I continued pleading with God.

As I listened to the rhythm of the heart machine, memories
of another lonely, discouraging time surfaced.

After my open-heart surgery, bouts of depression began.
Then a car accident left me battling insurance companies, stack-
ing doctor visits, and enduring more pain and more depression.
I finally had to give up building and refurbishing, which I loved

doing. I'd meet the guys for a walk and coffee at the mall, and that would help for a while.

Betty kept busy with the house, the girls' families, selling Avon, and caring for me. She couldn't understand, try as she would, what I was going through, why I was so hard to get along with. We fought, and I'm afraid I made life pretty miserable for her.

Taking long drives soothed me. Sometimes I'd just take off and be gone a few hours. Other times I was gone for a few days. I didn't learn until later that Betty and the girls prayed for me every time I left.

I don't remember what brought it on, but on one particular day, I took off for the mountains. I didn't know where I was headed, but knew I'd had enough of the struggles. At some point I pulled off near the top of a mountain pass. I looked over the mountainside. I stood there for some time, thinking, wondering, and praying . . . and in the quiet I heard my name.

"Bill."

I jumped and looked behind me—nothing. I leaned over the edge, searching. No one was there. Maybe behind the truck. I stooped to look under it.

Again—*"Bill."*

I dashed behind the truck, walked all the way around it. Nothing—no one was there.

It's just my imagination, I thought, *maybe the wind in the trees?*

"Bill!"

Was there a person down the road? Twisting and shielding my eyes from the sun, I looked for someone in the distance—but I knew the voice was right next to me.

"Where are you? Who are you? What do you want?" I asked.

"Bill, I'm not finished with you. I've still got work for you."
Deep inside, my heart knew what my head was still trying
to figure out. His voice was strong and clear. I couldn't see
Him, but I knew God was talking to me. He was right beside
me. *Talking to me!*

I stood thinking for quite some time. I realized I had a wife
who loved me. I had five beautiful girls who had husbands and
children—all who loved me and relied on me.

We were a lucky family—with health, love for one another,
and from time to time new babies. God wanted me to share
that. We were blessed. He had plans for us, and I was in the
middle of those plans, if only to tell the stories and remind
others of God's blessings.

I couldn't get back in the truck and turn it toward home fast
enough. I wanted to tell Betty and the girls, wondering if they'd
believe me. It was hard to believe myself that I had heard the
voice of God.

My mind returned to my hospital room. The mountain
memory kept me going most of the time. But these constant
visits to the hospital, each time leaving me weaker, seemed too
much to handle.

Something warm and comforting touched my arm. "Hi, Bill.
My name is Grace. I'm your nurse tonight. I just wanted to
see how you are doing." She paused. "You seem to be restless.
How can I help?"

She checked my temperature and read the monitors. Her
hands smoothed the covers and the wrinkles from my sheets.
Helping me raise my head, she fluffed my pillows. "Would you
like another pillow or blanket?"

"I don't think so. My back hurts, and I can't seem to turn
my mind off."

I was relieved to have her there. Her presence made me feel more comfortable.

"That's natural. You've been through a lot. I've got some time. Would you like a back rub?"

She helped me roll onto my side. She took out the lotion in my bedside table and talked as she rubbed it onto my tired, achy back.

"Would you like to tell me about your family?"

I told her about meeting Betty in grade school and how I used to torment her. "She wore her hair in pigtails and I loved to tie them in knots."

I told her about how her parents felt about me as a result of those stories. "Later, they wouldn't let her go out with me. But love won out, and we have a great family and have been married nearly fifty years."

I told her about my girls and their families, explaining the twenty years between my oldest and youngest. I told stories about all the kids and how happy I was when they were around.

"It sounds like you have a lot of reasons to enjoy life," she said. The tenderness in her voice and the gentle rotating hands seemed to sense all the places that ached, inside and out. As I drifted off to sleep, my mind traveled back to that mountain and God calling my name.

The next morning, I woke up feeling better. I wanted to find Grace and thank her for calming me and helping me sleep. When they brought my breakfast tray, I asked, "Is Grace still here? I'd like to thank her for last night."

The young man gave me a puzzled look. "I don't remember a Grace," he said.

"She was my nurse last night, and she helped me to relax and get to sleep."

Again, he looked puzzled. "Maybe she just works different hours than I do. I'll check."

Later, when the morning nurse came in to check my vitals, I made the same inquiry. "We don't have a nurse here named Grace," she answered.

"Would you please check for sure? Someone gave me a back rub and made me feel so much better last night. She had light brown hair tucked under her cap. She wore a white uniform."

Amy, the morning nurse, looked at me and shook her head. Later she came back in, "Bill, there was not a nurse named Grace anywhere in this wing, not only last night, but on any of the staff lists. Besides, we haven't worn white caps and uniforms for nearly twenty years."

I was able to go home from the hospital a few days later. Even as I recovered and began to feel better, I was not able to stop thinking about Grace. She was the answer to my prayer on that dark, lonely, scary night.

My Only True Security

ANNA M. GREGORY

Honey, they laid me off," Daniel said, a sheepish look on his face. "There's not enough work. I'll have to find another job."

I did not want to believe his words, but somehow I responded positively. "It will be all right. We'll manage." I hugged him and searched his face for assurance. Five precious boys to feed—we'd figure out a way to do this.

Day after day, Daniel came home after job hunting, stomped into the living room, flipped on the television, and muttered, "Nothing, absolutely nothing."

Week after week, he searched. Jobs were scarce. The interviewer at one job declared Daniel overqualified. Another interviewer declared him underqualified.

I worked part time, but my salary didn't pay all the bills. Each week after we squeezed out grocery money, very little was left.

One day, as we pondered what to do, frustration overwhelmed me. My sweet husband's eyes searched mine as I clenched my teeth.

"It won't help," he mumbled. "Anger won't solve this." He cleared his throat. "We need to sell some things."

"What could we sell?" I countered.

His eyes dropped.

"The expensive glassware your dad left you. We could sell the pictures on the walls." He motioned to them. "Some of the furniture, other stuff we can do without."

I cried as I realized we must sell our possessions so we could eat, so we pay the light and water bills. It hurt, but I agreed.

Early the next morning, I started cleaning out cupboards, pulling out things we could do without, taking pictures from the walls. I set up tables outside, made a rummage sale sign, and prayed, "God, I don't want to part with my things, but we need to eat. Oh, God, what should I do?"

As though God wasn't listening, I saw car after car pull into my driveway. I could scarcely breathe as people bought my possessions, things I treasured.

I can live without these, I told myself.

I didn't cry until I sold my special picture of Jesus. As long as that picture sat on the small table beside me, I felt God's presence. After I sold that picture, I felt destitute. I knew God cared, but it felt like everything was being swept away.

At times, I couldn't see or feel God. Sometimes I grew angry because He didn't answer my tear-filled prayers. And yet, most of the time, I found myself praying more and leaning on God more. There simply was no one else to lean on, only God. Prayer was my lifeline. I cried out to God, hoping He would answer.

A week later, I discovered we did not have the money to pay the light bill. Thankfully, it was summertime, but no lights? And how would I wash our clothes? If I had enough money, I could go to the laundromat, but how I hated that thought. Washing clothes for a family of seven was not easy. The thought of lugging those clothes somewhere filled me with dread.

That night, I dropped to my knees, praying desperately.

The next morning, I approached Daniel. "Honey, we don't have the money to pay the light bill. They'll shut our electricity off in a few days."

"It will be all right. We'll make do." Wrapping his arms around me, he held me tight as I cried.

That next day, I caught the first glimpse of God's wondrous, miraculous care. When I reached into the mailbox, I expected more bills I could not pay. Instead, I found a letter with a check.

"I felt compelled to send this to you. I hope it helps," the person had written.

I read the check amount twice. It was the exact amount of our light bill!

I cried with joy as I contemplated God's provision. Maybe things would get better.

The next day, I headed for the store to buy a few things for supper. As I walked, my mind whirled. We'd missed several house payments. Could we ever catch up? It would take a miracle to do so, but God did miracles, didn't He?

Gathering my purchases, and rounding up the boys, I headed for home.

As I stepped into the house, I reached into my pocket and discovered three packages of Kool-Aid. I hadn't bought them, because I wasn't sure I had enough money. I realized one of my sons had placed them in my pocket—he had wanted Kool-Aid, and I'd told him no. If only I had paid attention! Now I would have to go back and pay for them, since we'd taken them out of the store. But how? We had no money left.

I dug around the house, searching for change. It was another miracle that I actually found enough change to pay for the Kool-Aid.

I cornered the son who'd taken them. "Son, I'm going back to the store to pay for these, and you're coming with me to apologize for stealing."

That night as I prepared supper, tears fell like rain. It broke my heart that my sons wanted simple things we couldn't afford.

At supper, Daniel took my hand in his. "Honey, we need to apply for public aid so we can feed the boys."

I dropped my head. It was the ultimate disgrace and humiliation to find you couldn't feed your children by your own hands.

Going to the public aid office was like visiting a foreign country. The woman at the reception desk was kind. The next woman I met, the one who would decide whether or not to help us, was horribly rude and uncaring. She informed me that my husband had not been wise to quit his job.

"My husband did not quit his job. He was laid off," I replied.

"No, it says here on this form that he quit."

"Well, he didn't," I insisted.

She rolled her eyes. Still, she processed my claim and approved us for food stamps. At the grocery store, people glared at me as I pulled out the food stamps. I wanted to run and hide, but I couldn't. My sons needed to eat.

For several months, we had been running on empty. The final straw came in a formal letter that announced, "Pay your back house payments or we will foreclose."

I surveyed our huge lovely home, the large yard with the apple trees and beautiful giant pine. Tears filled my eyes at the thought of leaving, but I knew it was useless. We would have to leave. We soon received another miraculous glimpse of God's abiding love. God was slowly moving mountains for us.

A week after the devastating foreclosure letter arrived, Daniel ran inside shouting, "I've found a job. It's fifty miles from here, so we will have to move." He stopped. "I know you want to stay, but we can't keep the house. We can't begin to catch up on the payments, and the job doesn't pay enough to drive the distance."

The town we moved to was nice enough. The house we rented was small, cramped, and not so nice—but it was affordable.

I hated the change and yearned to go home. Occasionally we drove past the old house. It sat empty, abandoned. In my mind, I pictured the day we would move back. I was sure God could arrange that for us.

How surprised I was the day I drove by and the house was gone. It had burned to the ground. No pine tree, no apple trees, nothing. I was devastated. So much for my dreams and prayers to return there!

Time passed and lots of prayer before I saw the next miracle. I finally realized that God was pulling me from my comfort zone and turning my life around. He was giving me options. I could decide that I would survive and grow in grace or I could moan and cry over the past.

Even with Daniel's new job, it was still tough to make ends meet, so I looked for a job. Trusting that God knew what He was doing, I applied for a job at the local hardware store. It was a good match for my skills, so I hoped and prayed.

"I'm sorry, we don't have any openings," the owner said.

I fell to my knees that night and prayed again. "God, I need a job, any job."

Miraculously, two days later, the hardware store owner called and asked if I still wanted a job. One of their employees had decided to retire. I was ecstatic.

With both of us working, we settled into another house, and found our lives coming back together.

Again, God gave me a miraculous glimpse of His love. Our sons settled in at school. Change had not been easy for them, either.

One of our sons deeply wanted to move back to our former town. He let us know how he felt time after time. But after many prayers and tears, all of the boys, even the one who wanted to go back home, finally made new friends.

Like mist clearing from a field, it took me a while to see what God was doing. God gave us each of the houses we lived in as a place to make cherished memories. Those homes were gifts to be enjoyed for certain seasons.

God showed me that no matter where we lived, He would be with us. With each move, He lifted me from my safe world and led me into the real world. I felt God's touch on my heart as He showed me that He, my God, is my only true security.

So far during my life, God has led me through numerous new paths. Some of them I scarcely endured. But if I look hard enough, and listen carefully and prayerfully, I can always see miraculous glimpses of God's ever-abiding love and care.

Three Days to Live

VIRGINIA ROSE FAIRBROTHER

Thirty-seven years. That's how long my husband served as a pastor. But only a month after he left the pulpit, David had become deathly ill as a result of an auto-immune condition.

In the following months, he deteriorated to the point of barely being able to function. He couldn't remember how to spell the simplest words. His hand-eye coordination resulted in his writing becoming the tiniest scrawl. He shuffled from bed to the couch, bumping into walls, and dozed most of his days away in his favorite chair while we waited for the liver transplant team to let us know that a donor liver was available. The wait seemed endless!

Finally, we got the call from Vancouver General Hospital, letting us know it was time to fly there for the transplant. We were ecstatic!

In the intensive-care unit (ICU) after surgery, our family was overjoyed to see David pink-skinned instead of yellow. Hundreds of people had prayed for this day, and we received emails expressing joy and relief as we all thanked God for this precious gift of life.

Three weeks after the transplant, David was well enough to go "home" to our rented apartment in Vancouver, where we were to live for three months post-op, since our real home was too far away. David was on top of the world, but an even bigger test of our faith was right around the corner. Within twenty-four hours, David was rushed back to the hospital with bleeding, and ended up in the same room he had just vacated. How demoralizing! He was released within a few days.

A week later, David was again taken to the hospital by ambulance, this time with massive internal bleeding. Health-care professionals performed multiple tests to determine what was wrong, but they could not find the cause and could not stop the bleeding.

David went into shock and was eventually put on life support. During the final twenty-four hours before yet another surgery, he received twenty-seven units of blood—one and a half times the normal amount of blood in the body! The situation was critical. The social worker told me David was in danger of dying and to notify our family.

Once again, our three children flew in from out of town, arriving just in time to say their final, anguished good-byes to their unconscious father as he was wheeled away to the operating room. As we sat yet again in the ICU waiting room, we were very conscious of being held up by hundreds of prayers, and we were intensely aware of God's presence in the room with us.

When the doctor came out after the six-hour surgery to talk to us, he told us the main problem was that an aneurysm in the hepatic artery had burst, causing the massive bleeding. He informed us that the situation was tenuous at best.

David hovered between life and death in the ICU, so swollen from all the fluid pumped into him that he could not move any part of his body. And he couldn't talk because of the ventilator in his mouth.

"We are amazed he survived. It is quite incredible!" one doctor said with tears in her eyes. The hospital staff began to refer to him as the Miracle Man. Of course, we knew David had survived only due to the grace and power of God. He was the Great Physician who alone could heal David if that was His plan.

Five days later, David was transferred to the solid organ transplant ward, but developed pneumonia and was taken back to the ICU, much to our discouragement.

Fifteen days after the second surgery, David awoke with excruciating pain, his blood pressure dropping—and the fight was on again to save his life!

Two months after the initial surgery, our youngest daughter and I were summoned to attend a conference with five doctors where we were told that 60 percent of David's new liver had died overnight from a lack of blood supply, likely due to a clot in the artery. The only way he would survive was to get a new donor liver, and they estimated he had three days to live! David was immediately put on a Canada-wide urgent transplant list.

A couple of days later, David lay sleeping in the ICU while our oldest daughter sat by his bed. At 3 a.m. the nurse told them a second liver was available!

Our son and I had gone to the hotel late that evening for a rest, but I was lying awake, tossing and turning in bed, alternately praying, but then despairing that a donor liver would not be found in time. I wept and begged God to spare David's life once more.

Suddenly, at 3:30 a.m., a lamp at the other end of the room switched on suddenly, flooding the room with light! Amazingly, I was not the least bit afraid. Instead, I thought: *There is light at the end of the tunnel.*

I felt as if God was saying to me that He would light the way and that David would survive. Feeling reassured, but still somewhat in disbelief, I got up, turned off the light, and immediately fell into a peaceful sleep, murmuring a prayer of heartfelt thanks to God.

Toward morning, when our daughter called with the tremendous news that a donor liver had been found, I was overjoyed! When I arrived at the hospital and told my husband what had happened with the light, he started to cry. He said that right after he was told about the liver at 3 a.m., he asked God for a sign that everything would be okay. It seemed clear to us that God was saying, "I will light the way before you and I will bring you through this."

As David was wheeled to the operating room on November 11, just three days after his transplanted liver began to die, our family had an overwhelming sense of peace and confidence that he would live. When the doctor came out after the second six-hour surgery, he told us that David would not have survived much longer.

Unbelievably, David developed internal bleeding the next day, and on November 13, another six-hour surgery had to be done, although the cause of the bleeding was never found. It was David's fourth major surgery in forty-nine days!

Our youngest daughter and I were alone in the waiting room, waiting for the surgery to be finished, feeling lonely and overcome with emotion, when we both spontaneously started singing the same praise song.

God touched our hearts and filled us with His peace, reassuring us that He was in the room with us, and that He was with David in that operating room. Miraculously, the bleeding stopped on its own the following day.

While everyone was euphoric that David had survived this trauma, a difficult time lay ahead as his body struggled to heal. He had lost thirty pounds. Often it seemed there was little progress, but he was continually winning small battles just to stay alive. Everything was a struggle for David, but nurses called him a fighter and constantly encouraged him. The occupational therapist said, "Think of this time as similar to learning to ride a bike. Right now, you're using training wheels."

Our daughter quipped, "But you've been run over by the bike!"

Finally, after five long months in Vancouver, we drove back to our home six hours away. David had high hopes of a fast recovery in familiar territory.

It was a long, difficult year for us, however, with many ups and downs. At first, David was too weak to even step into the shower alone. He only weighed 108 pounds. He couldn't put his own socks on. He had no energy. Nothing tasted good. He only ate because he wanted to live. Sometimes God seemed far away.

As we, and countless others, continued to pray, the Lord worked His miraculous healing in David's body. He gradually regained his strength, and after some months he began to write his transplant story to encourage himself and others.

You cannot go through a journey like this without learning some profound spiritual lessons. I learned that nothing is too hard for God. When things seemed hopeless to me, God gave hope and whispered, *"Trust me."* When my strength was gone, God carried me.

Above all, I realized afresh that God is only a prayer away, and He delights in the cries of His children. David could not have survived the trauma had it not been for the grace of God in answer to all the prayers. He is truly a God of miracles!

Against All Odds

MARYBETH MITCHAM

I was only seventeen when my husband and I learned something was very wrong with our unborn baby. The ultrasound revealed gastroschisis—a congenital disorder that keeps the unborn child's abdominal cavity from correctly closing, allowing for a large portion of the intestines and possibly other internal organs to protrude from the abdomen through a small hole.

When the doctors first told us about the deformity, they strongly encouraged us to end the pregnancy because the prognosis for our child's survival and quality of life were grim. They stressed that the child would probably have severe cognitive defects, which would cause developmental delays and a lack of adequate physical mobility—that is, if the baby survived birth and post-birth surgery.

Despite the desperate warnings, my husband and I chose to continue with the pregnancy, knowing God was ultimately in charge.

Not surprisingly, I prayed fervently during the rest of my pregnancy and faced my fears that God's answer to my pleas would be one I did not want to hear. I knew God could work miracles—I had experienced unexplainable answers to prayer many times. But I also knew His ways are not our ways (Isaiah 55:8–9), and that in His omniscience, sometimes His bigger plan includes our walking through dark valleys and not seeing the answers we want.

Thankfully, my husband and I were part of an extremely supportive church community, which committed to pray not only for our child's miraculous healing, but also that God would keep His hand on that precious life, bringing all of His plans for her to fruition.

When every weekly ultrasound showed the mass of intestine still outside the abdominal cavity, causing my hopes to plummet, my church family's continued faith and prayers provided the support that kept me believing for a miracle.

At week thirty-two of my pregnancy, my baby stopped moving, so an emergency C-section was performed. When the doctors lifted my daughter's flailing body, enraged cries emanated from her tiny lungs. I knew that even though God had not healed her before she was born, He had given her a fighting spirit—one she would need to survive the challenges ahead.

Although we had been cautioned that it could take months for all of the intestines to be placed back into our daughter's abdomen, the surgeon was able to place the entire mass—which spanned our daughter's shoulders down to her knees—back inside her underdeveloped body in one surgery. The surgeon said he didn't know how to explain what had happened; he could only say that it was a miracle.

The prayers did not stop for our daughter's continued well-being, health, and safety.

Even though her intestines had been placed inside her body during that one surgery, our daughter still needed to stay in the Neonatal Intensive Care Unit (NICU) for an indefinite length of time to give her the best chance at healing and thriving. Every single visit included prayer for God's angels to continue to protect our daughter, and for all of the potential physical and developmental concerns that the medical professionals still had to address.

Our daughter had been in the NICU for about a month, slowly and steadily healing and growing stronger, when I noticed that fewer babies were around my daughter each time I visited. At first, I thought they had improved and were simply being transferred to a level of less intensive care.

However, I knew something was wrong one day when I saw a man with a canister on his back with a hose leading to an instrument in his hand. As he scanned the NICU, he talked in low tones with a worried-looking nurse. When I asked the nurse later what was going on, she said it was part of the hospital's normal procedures.

I didn't buy it.

The next morning, a staff member met me outside the NICU doors to tell me my daughter had been moved to another floor. I was so excited that she could leave the NICU that all thoughts of the mysterious man fled from my mind.

Two weeks later, as I was getting my daughter ready to be discharged, I ran into a NICU nurse. After we chatted about my daughter's improvement, I mentioned the man I had seen in the NICU. The nurse nervously told me that she wasn't supposed to talk about it.

But then she told me something that floored me.

When I left the NICU the day that I had seen the man with the canister on his back, she had just started her shift. Right after I left, she noticed a nurse she had never seen before, so she assumed she was a new hire. That nurse cared solely for my daughter, hovering over her through the entire night, softly singing to my baby.

The next morning, as soon as my daughter was transported to the other nursery, the nurse disappeared. When the NICU nurse checked the security cameras to try to identify the disappearing nurse, there were no images of any nurse near my daughter all night.

Around a month later, I learned that a pathogenic bacteria had been introduced into the NICU and had been responsible for the severe illnesses and even death of some of the other babies. As a precautionary measure, the remaining babies were moved to another section of the hospital.

That fateful night, some friends from church had felt urged to go to the hallway outside of the NICU and pray for God to send His angels to guard my daughter. These sweet people faithfully prayed all night long for my daughter's safety.

My daughter lived and thrived while those around her became ill and some died. I truly believe God honored the prayers of our friends by sending an angel—the nurse who was invisible to the NICU's cameras—to guard over my daughter, protecting her the last night she spent in the NICU.

That is not the end of the story, though. My daughter is now eighteen and is more vivacious than anyone I have ever known.

Despite the medical staff repeatedly cautioning that she would suffer developmental delays, my daughter met each milestone early. When she not only walked but also ran at the age of ten months, I knew God truly had miraculously healed her. Despite warnings that she would suffer ill health and would probably have to return to the hospital many times, she did not even develop as much as a sniffle. She has retained that imperviousness to pathogens throughout her entire childhood, only requiring annual well-child checkups.

Despite predictions that she would not be able to perform activities requiring excellent gross motor skills, she won the Presidential Physical Fitness award many times, has excelled in any physical activity she has attempted, and recently toured in Ireland with her Irish Step Dance group, performing intricate and challenging footwork.

Despite concerns that she would be cognitively challenged, she has excelled academically, completing an advanced high school course load and learning to speak and read Hebrew—for the fun and challenge of it.

Despite the warnings that she would not be able to exhibit high-level creativity, she has won awards for her art, plays the guitar, and oozes thespianism. Despite counsel that the dual factors of prematurity and being raised by very young parents would stunt her emotionally and make her unable to relate to others, my daughter tenaciously pursues justice and has a sacrificially compassionate heart.

Looking at this beautiful young woman, I know for a fact that God answers prayers and works ongoing miracles.

A Return to Sanity

EVELYN RHODES SMITH

I leaned against the wall outside the operating room door. Dr. Staats had said my father was unlikely to survive surgery, and even if he did, liver cancer would take him in a few days. I secretly praised God that years of agonizing care for my mentally ill father were about to end.

In two hours the door opened and the doctor emerged—I knew that ear-to-ear-smile would not be good news to me. It wasn't. He said my father did not have liver cancer. His problem was a ruptured gall bladder, and the infection had spread.

"I've removed it. He's going to be fine," he said.

A ton of bricks fell on me. I slid to the floor, sobbing. Did God not care for me at all?

Dr. Staats didn't know that during the Great Depression my father had deserted our family. Twenty years later, he showed up in my life again—but severely mentally ill. The courts had declared Dad incompetent. The doctor didn't know he had been in and out of our state mental hospitals a dozen times or that my father had tried to kill several people, and that I had prayed desperately for our loving God to remove him from my life. How could I endure any more horrors of caring for an insane father?

The doctor misinterpreted my reaction. He thought I was relieved to hear that my father would live. He lifted me to my feet and led me to a chair. Sitting beside me, he put his arms around me and let me cry on his shoulder. He tried to encourage me. "There, there, now, everything will be all right. Your father is fortunate to have a daughter who cares for him so much."

The more he talked, the more I cried. I completely lost it when he added, "Your father will live a good long life."

All that afternoon, memories of visits to mental hospitals played in my mind. There were no medications in those days to treat paranoid schizophrenia. Dad had welcomed the electric shock treatments because they temporarily stopped the voices in his head telling him to kill others. By the time he entered Staats Hospital, Dad had endured more than one hundred shock treatments. None stopped the voices for long.

Usually my husband, Ted, went with me to the mental institutions to visit Dad. One time, however, I drove alone fifty miles to Huntington State Hospital. When I arrived, I learned Dad and four other men had attacked people at the mental hospital that morning. The men had been put in isolation.

Not understanding what I was getting into, I asked to see Dad. A guard took me to the top floor. The elevator doors opened, and I stepped into a bare room. No furniture, no draperies at the windows. Just bare floors.

Five men sat on the floor, each with one hand chained to the wall behind him. They wore little, if any clothes, and were wild-eyed and crazy. My father was in the middle.

"I'll return in five minutes," the guard said, as I heard the elevator doors close behind me. Numb with fear, I stood frozen in place. Dad raised his free hand and waved for me to come closer. The other men glared at me.

"We've misbehaved," Dad said. "They won't keep us up here for long."

No words can explain the terror I endured until the guard returned. I could barely walk when I went out the front door to my car. I drove up old Route 60 toward Charleston and stopped midway at a roadside picnic table, where I collapsed, vomiting, and with a severe migraine. I finally regained control enough to drive home. When Ted came home from work, he found me with an ice bag on my head. Years later, I still relive that experience through occasional nightmares.

Hospital visits during Dad's eighteen years of mental illness were just part of the problem. When he was out on probation, he was a constant danger to his neighbors. Pretending to be a calm, religious man, he would fool them into trusting him.

The odd thing was that when asked, my dad readily admitted his intentions. Since I was responsible for Dad, my call to the sheriff's department would send the deputies after him. Dad would relay the latest "message from God," and the deputies would return him to the mental hospital. That scene had been repeated a dozen times since he had shown up on our doorstep.

At one time, a three-year-old girl lived with her mother in the house next to him. Dad told us that God had told him the little girl was the cause of all his mental problems, so he should kill her. I contacted the mother to warn her to keep her little girl away from him.

"Mr. Rhodes would never hurt anyone," she argued. "In fact, he baby-sits my little girl, and she loves him. I'm going to have my neighbors sign a petition to keep you from sending him to a mental institution!"

"Why don't you ask Dad if he intends harm to your child? You will hear it from him," I suggested.

When she asked, Dad admitted his plans. "God told me your little girl was coming in my house in the mornings and turning on my TV set! That's why I have to kill her."

As I sat outside of the operating room door, all of the horrors filled my mind. I could not cope with it any longer.

When Ted came to the hospital that evening, I told him Dad was still with us. When we saw Dad, Ted and I noticed his eyes looked unusual. He was calm and smiling. On the way home, Ted said, "Something is different about your dad's eyes. . . ."

As the days passed, his expression was still different from what I'd ever seen before. Calm, easygoing, he laughed and smiled a lot—which he had never done before—and he was pleasant. During previous years, his eyes had darted here and there, never settling down to look us straight in the eye. At our visits now, his attention focused on us. He was clearly looking at us through different eyes.

Dad was in the hospital for two more weeks, a total of forty-two days. His bill was over $3,000. It took three years, but Dad paid it himself out of his social security disability check.

Paranoid schizophrenia is caused by an inherited gene and is incurable. Therefore, it took a while for me to realize that

God had healed my father—totally and completely! Body and soul. Dad had been mentally ill since his early twenties. He had been declared legally insane by the Kanawha County Courts and spent eighteen years in and out of both Spencer State and Huntington State Hospitals. I could hardly believe it.

I finally accepted that God had performed a miracle in my father's life. Before surgery, he had gone to sleep insane. He awoke sane. When Dr. Staats became aware of the circumstances, he called it a miracle and reported it to the mental health department.

I had never prayed for my dad's healing, because I thought it was impossible. Yet despite my lack of faith, God gave a very disturbed daughter her father back. His ways are above and beyond ours, and sometimes hard to understand.

During the next two years, a dozen doctors who examined my father agreed it was a true miracle. None, including our family doctor, had ever seen anything like it.

The voices in Dad's head were gone. He realized the "god" he had listened to was not the true God. He found Christ as Savior and joined a church.

At age sixty-five, Dad applied for residency at Andrew Rowan Retirement Home in Monroe County, West Virginia. They accepted him, and he became a model resident. He was in charge of all the electrical equipment there and setting up and maintaining microphones and speakers in the main hall. Toward the end of his life, he was elected as a member on the governing board!

There's more to this story.

Several years later, Dad wondered if he could get his status as "incurably insane" removed by the courts. With that diagnosis, he was not allowed to vote, drive a car, or sign a legal paper. All legal documents had to have my signature.

I learned this kind of removal had never been done before, so I contacted a lawyer. When he heard my story, he became excited. "Let me check with my friends on the court and I'll get back to you," he said.

The director at the Andrew Rowan Home sent a legal form documenting my dad's fifteen years of sanity. He submitted a request that I should "contact the Kanawha County Court and ask to have the incompetency decision reversed."

The Kanawha County Health Department reviewed the medical information and wrote a letter asking that my father's sanity status be restored.

The Kanawha County Commissioner, whose office had declared my father incurably mentally ill with paranoid schizophrenia, agreed to change the status.

The judges heard the case and unanimously decided to reestablish my father's status as *sane*. My father could vote again. He could get a driver's license. He could sign his own legal papers—for the first time since he had been declared insane eighteen years earlier.

My wonderful Lord had answered my prayer. He did remove the mentally ill father from my life, but He replaced him with a new father who also became my brother in Christ!

Loving My Soldier

ELLEN FARRINGTON

On September 11, 2001, I watched my television in horror as the twin towers of the World Trade Center fell. My telephone rang. My husband, Paul, was calling to tell me we would need to talk when he got home from work.

That night, I learned my husband had suddenly joined the army that day.

Although I disagreed with his decision, our house went on the market, and my husband took a leave of absence from his work. My four-year-old daughter, four-month-old son, and I moved into my parents' home in another state while my husband went to the other side of the country for boot camp and training.

Those months of separation were filled with loneliness. Besides losing my daily time with Paul, I had lost our home and community—our church family and friends.

After Paul finished his training, we cautiously moved forward with our lives, waiting in fearful expectation for his unit's call to action.

That dreaded call came on Valentine's Day.

Paul packed his gear, kissed the children and me good-bye, and joined his unit. For six months, we all lived in limbo as we waited for the final orders that would send his unit from the mobilization staging grounds over to join the war efforts.

We waited.

And waited.

Finally, Paul's unit was ordered to stand down.

I was ecstatic, thinking my husband would stay safely at home.

But as soon as Paul returned, he told me he was transferring to the infantry so he could actively fight overseas.

Despite my disagreement, Paul got his transfer papers signed, completed infantry school, and prepared to join his new unit, which was already overseas.

Those weeks of pre-deployment preparations were a blur for me. I felt numb and desperately wanted to remain that way to avoid the excruciating pain I knew would fill me when the numbness wore off.

The night before he left for combat, Paul packed and repacked his gear, telling me over and over that he loved me, that he loved our children, and that he would be all right. I tried not to cry, knowing that tears would make it harder for him.

I failed miserably.

The next morning, my husband left for war.

Saying good-bye was horrible enough, but having to go back home and be strong for my children was even harder. I don't remember the drive home—only walking through the door and seeing my children's faces. Thankfully, my son was too young to understand what was going on, but my seven-year-old daughter was very aware. Her tears broke my heart.

The next months were awful. I did not regularly hear from Paul. Every communication blackout experienced by his unit caused me to live in terror that one day I would return home to find a notification that my husband had been killed in action. Every time I drove home from work, church, or errands with my children in the car, I would slow down before the last bend of the road in front of my house. I figured if a military vehicle bearing bad news was parked in front of my door, I could turn around and take my babies to someone who could shelter them while I returned to face my darkest fear.

I was living a nightmare.

I wasn't the only one living that bad dream. Despite my efforts to shield her, my daughter cried herself to sleep every night.

I couldn't blame her. I did, too.

There were some glimmers of light during those dark months. The night before he left, Paul had hidden little pieces of paper throughout the house, tucked in among the kitchen utensils, dresser drawers, and storage cabinets. Every time I read one of these love notes, I cried again.

Paul also wrote letters full of love for the children and me, including in these letters his requests for me to continue covering him and his squad in prayer. During those dark months, I did just that. I was not alone in my prayers, though. Friends, family, members of our church, and even total strangers prayed for the continued safety of Paul and the men in his unit.

As the months of war continued, my prayers morphed from requests for Paul's safety to continually begging God to let Paul come home quickly. I wanted my family together again.

Finally, I heard that Paul's unit was coming back to the United States. The families in his infantry unit were given a tentative return date and went through a debriefing of what to expect when the soldiers came back. In my excitement, I shoved this information to the back of my mind, telling myself it wouldn't apply to my family.

On New Year's Eve, at midnight, their unit finally returned. I jumped into Paul's arms, relieved that he was alive and whole and back with me. As he held me, I could only think that my husband was finally home. Everything would be all right.

I noticed that Paul was terribly thin, and that there was a new stillness to him. I firmly told myself it was of no consequence.

After his week of debriefing, Paul came home. Our daughter had made a WELCOME HOME, DADDY sign that she struggled to hold aloft when he arrived back at our house. My brave little girl melted into a tiny sobbing puddle when her daddy finally held her again.

Over the next week, our family experienced the "honeymoon" phase of reuniting. Little signs here and there suggested to me that all might not be well, but I tucked those premonitions into a corners of my mind, emphatically telling myself that all was now well.

All was not well, however. The next period of our family's life was the most challenging as we walked through some of the aftermath of war.

Paul was angry all of the time. I didn't know what to do to make him happy, and felt I had welcomed a stranger into our home. Home life was horrific, with a constant simmering fury that exploded without warning. Paul threw furniture across the rooms and punched holes into walls and through doors. He was constantly enraged and screamed at the slightest infraction.

He regularly had nightmares and would abruptly waken, unconsciously thinking and acting as if I were the enemy. Sudden noises made him jump. If I forgot to do something as simple as latching a window shut at night, the potential threat to our safety would send him into a rage, veins popping in his temples and tendons straining at his neck.

Although Paul never physically harmed the children or me, the situation was so awful that I did not know if I could stay with him.

I prayed, begging God for direction. I had promised Paul "for better or for worse" and "until death do us part," but did that still hold in the face of constant fear of what would happen if I said or did the wrong thing?

I was not expecting God's response to my prayers: *"You must show him what real love is by loving him unconditionally."*

At that point, I wanted to do no such thing. I was worn, weary, and heartsick. Hadn't I already gone above and beyond what anyone—even God—would have expected me to do?

No matter how many times I prayed, I heard the same response: *"You must show him what real love is by loving him unconditionally."*

So I tried.

Paul's unabated rage continued for so long that I reached a point where I simply could not continue.

After Paul had erupted in an exceptionally horrific way, I told God that unless something radically changed in my husband *that day*, I was going to leave and take the children with me.

Then, expecting that nothing with Paul would change, I packed a bag of clothing and supplies for my children and me, shoved it in a closet corner, and waited for the end of the day and my escape from the nightmare that now was my life.

A few minutes later, Paul came back into the house and apologized for his explosion.

I was stunned.

He had *never* apologized for losing his temper. I grudgingly told God I would stay. Things gradually changed at our home as the anger abated and the fury subsided.

Later, I found out that at the same time I had prayed my "this is it" prayer, my husband had heard an audible voice tell him that unless he changed right then, he would lose his family.

God's hand was on us the whole time.

Even though Paul was changing before my eyes, growing into the person I had always known he truly was on the inside, I was not changing for the better. I was bitter and resentful over what I felt had been lost years, and I didn't trust that any change in my husband would last.

Instead of the happiness I expected would accompany the prayed-for change in Paul, I was miserable. I became a version of the very person I had hated in my husband, spewing hurt and venom, erecting walls between my husband and me as I stewed in my bitterness. Even though I could see the hypocrisy in the situation, I felt justified, feeling that nothing that changed in my marriage would ever address the deadness I felt inside.

Walking through his own brokenness, Paul continued to patiently love me, praying for God to heal me, until God finally broke through my walls, uprooted my bitterness, and healed me.

Today, I love Paul more than when I first married him and thought that I knew what love was. Although we have faced some enormous hardships, through it all we have held on to each other and to God. Paul is a pastor today, openly telling how God has transformed his life to point others to the freedoms found in Christ.

Although we don't have a perfect marriage, I believe we have a good one because we have put God in the center of it, and because we have allowed our trials to refine us, showing the beauty that prayer and forgiveness can bring.

Paul and I are still married today as the result of answered prayers.

We have used our story to show people the freedom that comes from giving our hurt, anger, and bitterness to God and choosing to forgive. Only God can do that. Only He can bring such miraculous answers to prayers.

He has done that for Paul and me. He can do that for you, too.

The Two-Percent Life Experience

JAN APILADO

O Father God," I prayed, "why won't Corky listen to me? Will you please speak to his heart just like you're speaking to mine?"

For two long years the Lord had been pressing on my spirit: "*You're not where I want you to be. I want more of you.*"

Each time I had tried to tell my husband, Corky, of this insistent, restless spirit prompting me, he simply did not take me seriously. I felt very frustrated when he dismissed what God was telling me. He continued to go about business as usual, in the same life pattern we'd established while raising our family. Every time I told him of God's calling, he said, "Honey, we'll do more for God after we retire."

So during those years when God constantly leaned on me, my refuge was to lean right back on Him. After a while, I secretly referred to His call as my "God prod." My daily prayer to our

Father was that He would change my husband's focus from the business of making money to the business of honoring God. If He would do this, once again we would be of one accord.

Over the course of more than twenty-five years of marriage, Corky and I had been partners in all facets of life. We were a team in work, in play, and in parenting our four children. During the early years of our marriage, we started a new business: a sales firm with income based on commissions only. Our finances were so tight that Corky taught me how to hunt and fish. All of us loved our family time—camping out while we filled our game tags and sometimes caught our limit of fish for our winter meat supply. We relied on the trout, venison, elk, and bear stored in our freezer. The kids loved eating the food we caught as much as they loved camping out.

As our kids grew, God also grew our business.

Before we married, I knew Corky believed in God and lived a life of godly ethics, but I had wrongly assumed that he knew Jesus as his Savior. After I learned that Corky had never actually experienced a specific conversion, I told him just how much Jesus loved him. After seven years of marriage, Jesus awakened Corky's spirit. He opened his eyes to just how much he needed a Savior. This was one of the Lord's answers to my prayers, along with the prayers of an entire congregation.

So there we were in our fifties, with all our kids independent and building their own lives. Our business territory in the wholesale gift trade included five states of the Pacific Northwest. Corky was delighted that now, for the first time, I could travel with him in our motor home, which was custom-built as a showroom. Our business didn't feel like work because so many of our customers became our friends. They often shared with us both their blessings and their prayer concerns. Our days spent on the road together were such fun. The travel, good food, and fellowship with many Christians all gave us a very satisfying way of life.

But still the Lord continued to whisper, *"You're not where I want you to be. I want more of you."*

Summer business seasons were always exciting. We showed the new fall and Christmas merchandise at the gift shows the retailers attended. The travel schedule from the Salt Lake City show immediately to the Seattle show was always tight. In order to meet the deadlines, we had to drive straight through from Salt Lake to Seattle. We were both exhausted after five days of twelve-hour shifts, standing on our feet. Seattle was our last show on the summer circuit, so after that we could head for home in Oregon. We could hardly wait to sleep in our own bed again.

Corky was at the wheel and had been unusually quiet, but I didn't think too much of it. We were both so tired. As we drove on Interstate 84, about fifty miles east of Portland, Corky suddenly asked, "What would you think if I tried to get into seminary?"

At first I found it hard to believe he was actually speaking these words. Then my quiet response was "Praise God; it's what I've been praying for!"

Then nothing more—no words, not a sigh, not a sound, nothing—came from his mouth. I watched silently as his body sank down into his seat. He kept his eyes fixed on the road ahead. I felt as though an eternity had passed as I waited for what words might come next. But our silence went on for another ten miles. I dared not say anything, fearing he would recant his words.

Later he told me the thoughts that had been racing through his mind: *Oh, Lord, where did those words come from? I didn't really say that, did I? I couldn't have said that! That was not even a thought in my head. Oh, Lord, what can I do now? I can't disappoint you, God, and I don't want to disappoint Jan. And she said, "Praise God; it's what I've been praying for!" Lord, why, oh why, Lord, did I ever say that?*

After the ten miles had passed, I saw a rest area sign and said, "How about stopping there? We need to talk."

In the parking area, we discussed what had just happened and wondered what we were supposed to do. We determined that it had not been Corky's choice to say what he did, but that God was speaking directly through his mouth. Since we'd drive right past the Multnomah Bible College and Seminary campus, we decided to stop and check the enrollment requirements.

When we entered the admissions office, a very kind young man was on duty. After we explained our experience to him, and he knew Corky was a few credits short of his bachelor's degree, he filed Corky's enrollment application to the seminary graduate level program under a Life Experience category. After the paper work was completed, our kind Multnomah representative delivered a caution: "Let me warn you," he said, "only two percent of the applicants who apply under the Life Experience Program are accepted."

Somehow, we were not even fazed by the possibility of being denied admission, for it was God who had spoken. Our responsibility was to obey Him and let God take care of those two-percent odds.

We drove on to Seattle, conducted our business for the week, and headed back home to Oregon. When we arrived home, we sorted our mail piece by piece.

Aha! Here it is—an envelope from Multnomah Seminary.
Corky handed it to me. "Here, honey! You open it."

Lo and behold, he had been accepted into their graduate program.

When God moves—look out! Just three days later, Corky found himself sitting in class, dazed, and still wondering what on earth had happened!

But God did not stop there. He worked out all the major and minor details. First, He opened a two-percent-size door. Then, He provided for our every emotional and physical need. He answered every prayer all through this journey. We gave up our business, and God provided a good position for me. He gave Corky various jobs in nighttime security so he could study in between his duties.

Without our advertising it, God even sent us a buyer for our motor home showroom, so we no longer had the responsibility of the big payments. He also sent us friends to help fund the seminary tuition.

I so admire this man God gave me. He stayed the course in spite of the huge challenges of such a drastic life change. He had to relearn how to study. Thirty years had passed since his college days. During our three years in seminary, God clearly orchestrated all the events of our lives. We felt His love and His care so deeply that we said we were simply holding on to His shirttails. He was doing the rest.

Our God is a God of action! After Corky completed his seminary studies, we felt the call to serve as pastors to a few small rural church bodies. Today, twenty years after God spoke, we continue to serve Him as volunteer chaplains to retired military groups. All our praise belongs to Him, for it is by His grace that we have His peace.

He Gives His Angels
Charge Over Us

DELORES E. TOPLIFF

D elores, I'm terribly sorry, but while the children were playing hide-and-seek outside, there was an accident. Andrew's okay, but he hid behind shrubs by our cement wall, and when his brother scrambled over the top, we guess a loose block dropped down on Andrew's head."

As I listened to Lynda's voice on the phone, telling me about my son, I couldn't breathe.

"On his head? How bad is it?" I asked as I tried to calm the adrenaline suddenly shooting through my body.

"Surprisingly, it doesn't look that bad. He says to tell you he's fine. There's a one-inch cut that I think needs stitching. If it's okay with you, we'd like to get him thoroughly checked out. Our insurance will cover it.

"Meet us in the emergency room," she continued. "And it's the strangest thing. I had to call Wanda for your work number.

She said she'd had a dream that you and your kids were in danger, so she was already praying."

I don't remember shutting down the office equipment or rushing outside to hop in my car. I dodged traffic, going over the speed limit, hoping the police would stop me so I could ask for help to get to the hospital faster—but none appeared.

We hadn't lived in Dallas long. After I finished graduate school at the University of Missouri, the three of us—my sons Andrew, eight, and Aaron, six, and I—moved south to live near families we knew who were part of a family-friendly church about to open a small Christian school.

One of those families, Wanda and Bill Rankin, lived on a thirty-acre ranch outside of town with four nearly grown children. They assured me that they had lots of room and invited us to live with them until I found work and knew which part of town we should settle in. At that time, the whole Rankin family was packing for volunteer missionary service in the remote jungles of Colombia, South America.

Our family fit well with theirs. Bill was a gifted architect and lay pastor with a great sense of humor. He always put strangers at ease. Wanda was a tenderhearted Texan, who tucked my guys into her arms and heart as if they'd always been there. She sang so beautifully in her church and at home that I'm convinced angels stopped to listen. When people had prayer requests, Wanda stepped into action. Sometimes she even sang her prayers and the Scriptures. Her favorite song came from Zechariah 4:6: "Not by might, nor by power, but by my Spirit, says the Lord of hosts" (ESV). Her singing made us believe it.

My kids and I loved those days with this warm, welcoming family. After we first arrived, I worked temporary jobs to find one that would be a good fit. I wasn't in a great hurry since we were so happy in this home. Besides, I enjoyed helping Wanda prepare to move to South America.

As summer ended, the church's new school got off to a great start. My kids found friends and were invited to classmates' homes. The Nicholas family had two sons the same age as mine, so they invited my boys over for playdates. That's where they were after school that day while I was at work. All four boys had raced around the yard playing games. Andrew crouched behind a shrub in front of a six-foot retaining wall. His younger brother had climbed over that wall to hide behind it, but one cement block in the top row was loose. Without warning, it dropped straight down.

While driving, I phoned Wanda to thank her for praying.

"It was the strangest thing," she said. "I woke up from a nap, dreaming you and the boys were in danger. I'll tell you more when you get home, but I jumped up praying and shouting. I won't stop until we know everything's fine."

I cried as I swerved into the hospital parking lot and rushed inside. Lynda awaited me, looking pale, with my son Aaron and her kids at her side.

"Where is he?" I asked.

"Right there." She waved to the nearest curtained-off area. "I'll tell the doctor you're here. Our insurance is fine, but they need your paper work, too."

"Sure." I fumbled for cards as we hurried to reach Andrew. Lynda parted the curtain, and there my son sat on the edge of an exam table, just as a doctor was putting neat stitches in the top of his forehead.

I couldn't hug Andrew while the doctor worked, so I gripped his hand. "Thank God, you're alive," I half sobbed.

He squeezed my hand back, looking like he was afraid he was in trouble. "I didn't mean to get hurt, Mommy. And it's not Aaron's fault."

"I know, sweetheart."

Aaron grabbed me. "I couldn't tell it was loose. I shouldn't have climbed up."

I hugged him close. "All that matters is that you're both okay."

I turned to the doctor. "He will be okay, won't he?"

"Yes, I'm sure he will, and that's amazing."

The doctor tied the last knot. "You have quite a young man here. I hear a twenty-eight-pound cement block fell on Andrew's head. It could have killed him. I can't figure out why there isn't more damage." He gestured to the stitches. "Except for this cut near his hairline, X-rays don't show any problems. You should watch him for concussion, but otherwise, he's great—one very lucky young man." He patted Andrew's shoulder. "And the bravest eight-year-old I've seen. He didn't fuss at all while I stitched him up."

Andrew flushed with pleasure.

After the doctor finished and we were released, our joyful drive home included stopping for ice cream cones. When we reached the Rankins' house, Wanda told us more of her vivid dream.

"I didn't know what was happening, just that something was very wrong. I saw you driving somewhere with your boys in the back seat of your car. You got out to take care of something and the only place to park was on the edge of a hill. You were gone a minute, when the emergency brake failed and the car started rolling toward the edge. There was nothing between your car and the cliff so you started running but couldn't get there fast enough. That's when I jumped up, shouting prayers for God to keep you all safe. Next, I started singing, 'It's not by might, not by power, but by my spirit saith the Lord.'"

"Do you remember what time it was?"

"Yes, I looked at my watch. I was on my feet praying at 4:15."

My knees became rubber. "Lynda says the accident happened at 4:20. How did you know? How can I thank you for praying? I'm sure your prayers saved his life."

"I just do what God impresses on me, dear." She wrapped us in the warm hugs we needed just then. "He's the one watching out for you to send help when you need it." And thankfully God sends that help when others pray!

My Emmanuel Moment

HOLLY BLEVINS

I stood with my wet hands braced on the edge of the kitchen sink and looked up at the ceiling with tears in my eyes. I no longer felt God's presence. As much as I looked, I couldn't find Him.

We had stopped attending church, having watched every pastor and mentor we knew fall out of ministry. The disappointment had taken its toll on my faith and left me numb. I longed for the days when my faith was on fire, when I was passionately leading people to Christ and bringing the hope of the gospel to the lost. There was nothing that brought me more joy than witnessing people being reconciled to their Creator and being set free from sin.

Now that joy seemed like a vaguely recalled dream; I knew it had happened, but the details were a little fuzzy. Doubt had taken root and wound itself into my memories, causing me to wonder if my personal experiences were just a figment of my overzealous imagination.

I began to pray. I needed God to show me He was real. I knew I couldn't halfheartedly ask such a thing from God, that it needed to come from my heart. I looked toward heaven and simply prayed, "God, if you are real, and you are still here, please show me."

I did not believe God would answer me. I crawled into bed that night feeling no different and hopeless. Then I began to dream.

I dreamed I was sitting down, surrounded by people crowding me and shuffling past—their dirty sandals kicking up dust and barely missing my fingers that rested on the ground. The large white columns of the inner courtyard made it difficult to see, so I stood and moved in a little closer to get a better view of the commotion. A Roman centurion was going through the crowd and questioning each person. I became frightened and turned to leave, but then I saw Him. When you see Him, you know Him.

It was Jesus. He was behind me, sitting casually against the wall and looking out at the crowd. The soldier raised his voice, demanding the people tell him who this man was. They started yelling, "Blasphemer!" and all kinds of names.

I knew who He was. I knew He was innocent. I wanted to scream for Him to answer them, to put a stop to the false allegations! But Jesus didn't speak. He sat silently gazing out at His accusers.

When the Roman soldier had maneuvered his way over to me, he stopped. Looking directly into my eyes he said, "Who do *you* say this Jesus is?"

I walked over to Jesus, let my hair fall to cover my face, and sat at His feet. As I did, the story of a woman who had followed

Jesus just to be able to touch the hem of His garment flooded my mind, and I reached out and touched His leg. I was shocked to feel His hand rest on my head. I looked up into the gentlest eyes I have ever seen.

At once, my spirit was infused with supernatural peace, gratitude, and the joy of knowing and being known. His eyes pierced my soul so deeply that had I not known Him as my own, I would have been frightened.

I stood, shaking, but determined to speak to His accusers. In a loud and clear voice I answered them, "He is the King of Kings and the Lord of Lords. But His kingdom is not of this world, as you all fear. It is the kingdom of heaven. He alone can save you. He alone is our Savior and Deliverer from evil. He is who He says He is, the Son of the Living God, and I believe Him."

I looked into His gentle, sea-green eyes, and wished time would stop. His face began to fade as His Spirit spoke to my spirit. His soft smile was full of assurance.

As I woke, I knew this dream was a gift from God and a personal answer to my prayer—my very own Emmanuel moment.

Earlier that day, I had wondered if God would show me who He was by performing an unmistakable miracle or speaking audibly, but that night in my dream He did the *unexpected*. He allowed me to have a glimpse of His glory, face-to-face. He gave me the opportunity to proclaim once and for all who He is so that in every problem I face or trial I go through I can place my hope on the unchanging answer to the most important question: Who do I say He is?

Sometimes He sends His angels to protect and comfort His children or leads a dear friend to pray with and encourage us, but that day at the sink, Jesus heard my heart's cry and answered me himself. To see His face is to see hope and to know truth.

He is the Almighty God, Creator of the universe, and He will never leave us or forsake us. He is waiting to answer our prayers, but sometimes we are asking the wrong questions.

During faith-defining moments, the Holy Spirit is right there covering us with grace and mercy, leading us, guiding us toward Him. He knows our deepest needs, and He knew better than I did that what I needed was the strength to stand and declare who He is in my life. I have never been the same.

An Unexpected Gift

David Michael Smith

Ellen Knight decided she would do something about the one in six Americans who deals with hunger every day. She would fight back—at least for the needy residents on the lower Delmarva Peninsula near Berlin, Maryland. She campaigned to start a food pantry at her church, Holy Trinity Cathedral, and the parishioners warmly welcomed the idea.

Most of the donated food items were transported to the homes of hungry area residents, and occasionally visitors would come to the church for help. No one was denied. When pantry shelves started to empty, Ellen would stand up and make an announcement, and the faithful people of God would bring in more bags and boxes of nonperishable items to share with the less fortunate.

One anonymous parishioner wasn't sure what to bring in, so she purchased a gift card at a local grocery store and placed it in the box with a note that read, "Ellen, please use this to buy whatever is needed; God bless!"

Ellen held on to the card and forgot about it for several weeks. Thanksgiving and Christmas were approaching with their normal emphasis on food distribution. Everyone tends to think about food when the holidays roll around.

Again the pantry was bare, supply and demand out of balance, and Ellen solicited donations. And although the people of Holy Trinity again responded, she remembered the gift card.

"Lord, what should I purchase with this card?" she prayed, only a week before Thanksgiving. She didn't perceive an answer, but scheduled a trip to a chain store she seldom shopped at and trusted the Lord would lead her when she arrived. Ellen prayed daily and often, and she knew the Lord would respond sovereignly when the time was right.

After a busy day at work, Ellen headed home, exhausted and overwhelmed. Her mind was distracted. As she approached a busy intersection near the seashore tourist community of Ocean City, she sensed the Lord reminding her to turn at the light and visit the Food Lion storefront. She had forgotten completely, but with God's prompting, she made the turn, and a flood of energy returned.

"May your will be done, Lord," she prayed as she pulled into the parking lot.

Inside the store, she pushed the cart around, oblivious as to what to purchase. The building was busy with shoppers grabbing things off the shelves for the upcoming holiday. Finally she tossed in some boxes of Hamburger Helper, a few cans of vegetables and diced fruit, and some juice boxes for small children.

It wasn't much, and the randomly chosen items probably wouldn't expend the entire gift card.

"Why am I even here?" she asked herself, disappointed in her selections. Something didn't feel right. The church pantry had looked well-stocked again when she'd last visited it after Sunday worship, and the purchases in her cart really weren't necessities. Still she pressed on, looking for the exit to this spiritual maze she found herself in.

As she approached the checkout lines, she noticed a solitary woman in the express lane. Ellen's cartload was small and qualified for the same lane, so she stepped in line behind the woman who apparently was shopping for her own Thanksgiving dinner.

The cashier scanned each item and slid it down for bagging—vegetables, frozen yeast rolls, a container of mashed potatoes, a box of stuffing, some macaroni and cheese, a frozen pumpkin pie, and a small turkey. The woman looked stressed, unhappy, and maybe even a little frightened. Ellen thought, *She must've had the same kind of day I've had.*

After the last item was rung up, the cashier announced the total: "Fifty dollars." The woman seemed to balk, and Ellen suddenly felt a presence.

Again the cashier repeated, "That'll be fifty dollars, please. Will you be paying with cash or with a credit or gift card?"

The woman made no movement to produce the cash or a credit card. In fact, she appeared forlorn, distraught, panicky. There was an uncomfortable silence for what seemed an eternity.

"I prayed this morning," the woman finally said, pulling at a scarf wrapped around her neck. "I know this will sound crazy to you, but God answered my prayer. I asked for a Thanksgiving dinner for my family. We're broke, out of work, but God told me very clearly to come here to shop and that He would provide."

Ellen felt the presence of God nudging her; her mind and heart were racing.

"I'm sorry for your misfortune, ma'am, but I'll need payment or I can't let you exit with these groceries," the cashier replied firmly.

"You see," the woman started, "God said to come here and He'd provide a way. I came here in faith, but now I'm feeling a bit foolish . . . I am so sorry." She began to cry.

"Here, let me pay for your groceries," Ellen finally spoke. She handed the cashier the gift card, which was for the exact amount of the woman's purchase.

The woman praised God quietly, and hugged Ellen for her kindness. Ellen wept. The cashier was shocked, but he accepted the card and completed the transaction.

"Thank you," the woman cried as she held Ellen in her arms. "You are my angel, the answer to my prayers."

"No," Ellen replied with a smile, "I am quite sure you are mine."

My Dream Husband

LAURA L. BRADFORD

Please, God," I sobbed, "I know you can raise the dead. Could you please send my husband back to help me?"

It wasn't the first time I'd prayed that prayer in the six years since Jesus had called John home to heaven. I found it impossible to let go of my husband because he'd been my faithful hero, buffering me from the hardships of life.

It was wonderful to think that John had been set free from his sufferings caused by the increasing paralysis of multiple sclerosis. But whenever my life got complicated, I'd rattle heaven's gates again, begging God to send John back to help me.

"Lord, please?" I whined. "John would be able to handle this legal stuff so much better than I can."

The clock read 10:21 p.m. as I stared at the intimidating piles of paper work. They were growing taller and more confusing with the arrival of each day's mail. John's mother had passed away only a few weeks earlier, and I'd inherited the job of handling her estate. Her attorney was an honest, experienced family friend. But I couldn't understand all of his instructions and legal jargon. I wanted to understand. I wanted to do all the right things for Mom—to carry out even the least significant aspects of her will. Yet I felt intimidated by the enormity of the task.

I might have been less rattled if I hadn't been facing another huge battle. Only four days after Mom's funeral, a distracted driver in a large pickup truck had turned left immediately in front of my small car. The accident left me with another mountain of confusing paper work, since my car was nearly totaled and I suffered numerous injuries.

"God," I begged, ignoring my body's need for sleep, "John was the one with a master's degree in business. This stuff would be easy for him. Could you please, ple-e-ease send him back to me?"

I heard only the ticking of my wall clock, reminding me of the late hour and of Jesus' earlier encouragement to get my rest. After a few more sobs, I fell into bed and drifted into a fitful sleep.

Morning's light was subdued by cloudy skies as I filled my teakettle at the kitchen sink. Out of the corner of my eye, I caught movement. Despite the early hour, someone was walking along the sidewalk in front of my house. Turning to see who it might be, I dropped the kettle in shock.

"John!" I gasped.

My husband was hobbling toward the front door on the crutches he'd used during the early stages of multiple sclerosis. He looked remarkably young, not at all like the emaciated man who died in his mid-fifties. The handsome man approaching my door was John at about thirty years old. He wore his favorite outfit—a pair of 501 Levis and a brown T-shirt that accentuated the ever-present twinkle in his deep green eyes.

In a mix of delight and panic, I tried to smooth my uncombed hair. Gazing down in horror at my raggedy bathrobe and slippers, I cried, "No-o-o! I can't let that handsome man see me like this. I'm more than twice his age and . . . what will he think?"

Nevertheless, I raced toward the front door and flung it open for my beloved husband.

He stood on the doorstep grinning at me.

The only words I could muster were "Oh, John, you're a sight for sore eyes!"

He cocked his head to one side, looked me up and down for a few seconds, then said, "Well, sweetie . . . so are you."

While I chuckled, John stepped into the house. At least, I think he stepped in. Astonishingly, I felt him pass right through me like the wind through a net.

Without warning, I was swept into a joyous whirlwind of heavenly love, freedom, and peace. With my arms lifted high, flailing in the breeze, I tossed my head back and laughed aloud while I twirled in that heavenly realm. No longer aware of John, I desired only the presence of my heavenly Father.

When one of my arms struck the bed's headboard, I bolted awake. The clock read 3:08 a.m.

"John?" I called. My husband had vanished with the dream. Yet my mind still lingered in the delight of my heavenly encounter.

With heart pounding, I tried to distinguish the real from the imagined. Was it only a dream? Or had it really happened?

Regardless, God sent me a message through that experience. While I wondered why John had come to me on crutches, the Holy Spirit revealed what those crutches represented. If my husband were to return to earth, he'd have to face more suffering. Did I wish to see him endure more?

Absolutely not! John lives in that whirlwind of heavenly love, freedom, and peace. I would be selfish to insist that he return from a place of eternal bliss just to coddle me.

As my heart calmed, the path ahead became clear. I had to let go of John.

My compassionate husband didn't leave this earth without teaching me all he could about legal matters, finances, and the handling of estates, since he knew I'd face those things alone someday. He'd instructed me to lean on my "resource people," those who had the expertise to guide me through everything: lawyers for legal matters, bankers for money matters, and, of course, my Christian friends for matters of faith.

From professionals to friends, God had surrounded me with individuals who were poised to help. But best of all, God's Spirit is always with me, sovereignly guiding. All I have to do is follow.

In light of these revelations, I prayed, *Forgive me, Lord, for wanting John back rather than looking first to you. And thank you for setting my husband free.* With that, I lay back on my pillow and drifted into a peaceful sleep—something I hadn't experienced for a very long time.

A Heavenly Code Blue

JEFF ADAMS

On July 5, 2001, I flatlined during my second heart attack. I heard the monitor and turned my head to see the horizontal green line.

Does that mean what I think it means?

I thought the nurse closest to me might faint.

I don't know if she did. I don't have any specific memories of when I awoke. My wife, Rosemary, who stood at the end of the bed in the ER, told me what had happened next.

"They called, 'Code Blue. Code Blue,' and tilted your head down. But before the crash cart got there, you were back. They never used the paddles to shock you."

My first heart attack had followed what could have been my last supper. A delicious tender steak, baked potato, and salad would have been my demise—as is so often the case, especially for men.

That was in May 1998, when my daughter Meaghan was only three weeks old. I learned the digestive system uses enormous amounts of blood, which can overburden your heart.

The trigger of the second heart attack in 2001 remains a mystery. It was past our bedtime when I was feeling the pain and learned Rosemary had forgotten to pay a couple of bills.

"I'll take them to the offices and put them in the drop box so they'll be there first thing in the morning," I said. It was a good excuse to get out of the house. *I'll stop by the hospital. They'll tell me I'm fine. She'll be asleep before I get home.*

As happened before, in the ER, God spared my life.

Somehow, Howard, our pastor, found out about my ER trip and pounded on our front door. "Rosemary! Wake up!" She opened the door. "Jeff's at the hospital."

When Rosemary got there, an ER doctor broke the news. "He's having a heart attack. The drug is working just the way it's supposed to." The cardiologist seemed surprised but glad. And since I needed surgical intervention they couldn't provide in that rural hospital, he told Rosemary, "As soon as he's stable, we'll Air Evac him to Phoenix."

I was afraid. I'd begged my friend Howard to pray for me. "You know what to say." Then he left.

Oh, God, not again. I can't take this. Dear God, please forgive me.

When you can't breathe, all you can think is what I thought. *I don't want to die!*

Some people think dying wouldn't be that bad. If you believe in Jesus, you expect to go to heaven. No more sorrow. No more pain. No more suffering. Perfect body. And much more. Reminds me of an infomercial. All yours for the low cost of leaving this world. But I'm in no hurry to do that.

I'll have all eternity to spend with God. I'm needed here. I have a wife, a daughter, a church that needs me. People who want me. I didn't want to leave. But it wasn't up to me.

What about Meaghan? Who will teach her what she needs to know? Who will hold her? Who will sing to her and dance with her?

I recalled our first night together. I sat in the hospital nursery rocking her. Our dear friend Gwen, one of the nurses on duty, handed me a bottle. "She won't eat. She hasn't."

I rubbed the nipple across Meaghan's lips. She greedily gulped, but milk poured out and ran down her chin to soak her nightgown. "Gwen, I think the nipple is too big."

"How did we miss that?" Gwen took the bottle, traded out nipples and handed it back to me. Meaghan devoured the formula. I burped her, more by accident than expertise. We leaned back in the rocker. Soon Meaghan drifted off to sleep to the lullaby of my voice singing the lyrics she would know so well— "Jesus loves me, this I know, for the Bible tells me so."

God, I want to sing again. I want to hold my daughter. I know it's a selfish prayer, but please, God. Don't let it end like this.

The pain increased. I couldn't exhale. A heart attack has that effect. It's the opposite of crucifixion, when you can't inhale. I imagined what Jesus must have endured.

I'm sorry. I'm sorry. God, please forgive me.

I felt calm, tranquil, peaceful, at rest, not a care in the world. Only later did I learn that Pam, Howard's wife, had begun to "storm the gates of heaven." That's how she described prayer. To Pam and others in our church that she enlisted that night, prayer was something akin to D-Day—an all-out assault. I learned later that hundreds of people in other churches joined the fight for my life.

In the moment when I needed it most, God heard. He answered. He gave me His peace.

Does that mean what I think it means?

"Code Blue! Code Blue!"

No tunnel. No light. No welcoming committee. Nothing. Except serenity.

God answered my prayers. And the prayers of so many others. I know my wife prayed that July as she did in May three years earlier. "God, no. I didn't sign on to be a single parent. I'm not doing this by myself. Bring him back. Now."

I'm grateful that family and friends and neighbors and strangers around the world prayed for me, with me. God can save by many or by few. But I am especially comforted knowing God heard my plea.

Semper fidelis not only describes the Marines, it also describes God. Always faithful, God gave me what I asked for.

I'm not sure when I became aware of my surroundings again. Maybe it was later than night. Perhaps it was the next day or the day after or the day after that. It might have been morning. It could have been afternoon. *When* God answers a prayer isn't what we notice. I only knew I could breathe. My chest didn't hurt. I only knew that by the grace of God I wasn't dead.

After I was revived by someone besides the physicians, EMS personnel loaded me on a helicopter to the airport for another flight to Phoenix. Different hospital, different doctors. Same procedure. An angiogram became angioplasty in order to place multiple stents. The tiny collapsed scaffolds, when deployed, would lock open and support my weakened arteries at critical junctures.

I became gradually aware at some point that I was in an ICU room. The recurring hum of a small pump measuring my blood pressure. The familiar blip of a monitor graphing my heartbeats. The ping of an alarm to alert the nurses that I'd finished yet another bottle of whatever they fed me through an IV. I dozed on and off as the TV faded in and out. I barely noticed the soft padded footsteps of various personnel who checked on me. My environment served one purpose: rest. So I did.

I still do.

I rest in the goodness of God. And I pray. I'm thankful I don't have to be afraid. I pray others won't be.

The Prayer Stone

RAY STENNER, AS TOLD
TO JANICE RICHARDSON

Bill carefully placed the prayer stone with my name written on it under the altar of his church.

"This is for you, Ray," he whispered, "I pray that you will come to know Christ and give your life to him."

The church was under construction, and the members decided to put prayer stones under the altar. Then they held a special service in which they prayed for the people whose names were on the stones.

Bill was my business associate and friend. We had often discussed politics, Christianity, and faith. I had been exposed to Christian teachings in my home as a child, but once I left home, I left Christ behind. Although I did not know it, Bill prayed for me every day. He had no idea how badly I would need those prayers.

Two years later, on June 2, 2005, I was doing what I enjoyed most, coaching my two daughters (ages seven and ten) in soccer and spending time with them. Early the next morning, I woke up with a severe ocular migraine in my right eye. I headed downstairs to get some painkillers, when I suddenly collapsed and tumbled the rest of the way down the stairs. My wife, Colleen, ran down to see what had happened.

"My eye! My eye!" I cried.

Colleen called 911, but I was unconscious before she got off the phone. By the time the ambulance arrived, I was no longer breathing. The paramedics resuscitated me twice because I had physically died for a few minutes.

I descended into blackness, and my human sensations started to disappear. I felt my spirit emerge. An unbelievable presence of love and peace overwhelmed me, like a mother's love as she snuggles her child, as well as a fatherly presence of strength and security giving me the will to live.

"You must go back," I was told. *"It is not your time to die yet."*

This was the first of several miracles and answers to Bill's prayers that changed the direction of my life.

My condition was an aneurysm on my right optic nerve. A massive vascular hemorrhage filled the right side of my brain with blood, causing a serious brain injury. While I was in a coma, the doctor said I would probably not live through the night. I was put on life support with no brain activity.

Colleen gathered my siblings for final farewells and decided to disconnect my life support and donate my organs. But a neurosurgeon on call arrived and convinced my family to let him perform a surgery.

The surgery worked! I remained in a coma for a week to let my brain heal. When I woke up from the coma, I could not speak, but immediately wrote about my supernatural experience while in the coma.

The magnitude of my injuries from the aneurysm overwhelmed me. At the age of forty-four, I had partial paralysis on my left side, significant visual loss in my right eye, memory loss, and serious cognitive impairment. Having been a project manager and operations manager, I was devastated to know I would never be able to work or drive again. My former life had been literally ripped out from under me!

Learning to do basic skills again, such as taking care of my hygiene, walking, talking, and eating with utensils was physically and mentally exhausting. A month and a half after my aneurysm, I was transferred to the rehabilitation ward and enrolled in speech and occupational therapy and physiotherapy. Feeling the tremendous impact these disabilities had on my life, I developed severe depression and anxiety.

One night, I woke up to see a small woman with dark skin at the foot of my bed. She exuded a loving motherly presence similar to what I'd experienced in my coma.

"Don't worry. You're going to be okay. You are loved," she reassured me. *"Be strong. Be brave. You will get better."*

I felt a deep sense of peace and fell back to sleep. The next morning, anxious to find out who that woman was, I stumbled to the nurses' station to ask. They told me no one of that description worked there. I eventually understood that she was an angel sent by God.

With renewed determination, hope, and confidence, I worked vigorously in all areas of therapy and could soon walk with only a cane. By the end of September, my dream of being home with my family again seemed closer when I was granted weekend visits. I could not hold back my tears as my youngest daughter ran into my arms, crying, "Daddy's home!"

The girls and I spent precious moments just hugging each other. I had missed them so much. I truly cherished my involvement in their lives—reading with them, cooking, swimming, taking them to dance lessons, and coaching their soccer teams.

Unfortunately, Colleen did not receive me the same way. She resented having to care for a disabled husband and did not think I could resume my role as father and husband. Her words and actions were hurtful and made me feel abandoned. To help me deal with this, my psychologist helped me find a church close to my home. The first day I attended, I was overjoyed to be warmly welcomed by friends whose daughter I'd coached in soccer.

Reading my Bible and being part of a loving, supportive congregation helped me to grow spiritually. Unfortunately, the situation with Colleen grew worse. I felt worthless after a difficult Christmas—my depression deepened and I felt suicidal. I couldn't understand why God let me live after the aneurysm. I could not see a purpose for living.

On December 28, 2005, I prepared to end my life by jumping off a pedestrian overpass. Just before the fatal jump, my cell phone rang.

Through tears, I poured out my emotions to my friend.

"No, Ray! No! Can you go somewhere safe? Is there a motel near you?"

He talked me into checking into the nearest motel, at his expense, and promised he would meet me there in the morning. Upon checking in, I was even more surprised to see that the front desk clerk was a former business associate of mine.

He eventually helped me find a townhouse to live in near my girls. God's divine intervention saved my life for a second time. When I moved into the townhouse, Colleen refused to let me have visitation rights, saying my daughters would be unsafe with me. I was very lonely without my girls. At an all-time low and unsure of my abilities and life as a disabled person, I cried out to God, "Lord, I give you my life! My former life is gone, even my family! You are my only hope! Please direct my life and please bring me the family that I need!"

My sister offered to visit every second weekend so my daughters could stay with me. Through the help of friends, I hired a lawyer. Eight months after I moved into the townhouse, the courts granted me visitation with my girls. The assessment stated that I was a better father than many fathers without brain injuries! This was a breakthrough for me and wonderful times began again with my girls.

As the girls grew older, I got less time with them. My oldest daughter pulled away when she was fifteen. My youngest daughter still wanted to come but also pulled away when she started ninth grade.

Heartbroken and lonely, I prayed again for a family. I tried dating through Internet sites, but brain-injured applicants are not well received. After a nine-month relationship went sour, I believed I would never be able to have a relationship with a woman and decided that God was all I needed.

But God had other plans. I started attending a men's group at a different church and eventually started attending their Sunday evening services. Two months later, on October 21, 2012, I was taking Access taxi (a special transportation for disabled people) to the church and it stopped to pick up a woman, Rose, and her special-needs daughter, only a block from my house. We talked all the way to church and found ourselves looking at each other during the service. We talked more after church.

A few days later, I was reading the Bible in my living room. I glanced out my front window and saw Rose walking her dog in front of my house! I flew out the front door as best I could and surprised her with a hug. A few days later, Rose dropped a note in my mailbox, offering to help me rake my leaves. Unfortunately, her note slipped out and fell to the ground. Several days passed before I discovered it. I called her, and the romance bloomed from there.

Rose had been a single parent for many years. Raising a special-needs daughter, coupled with love for Christ, gave her a compassionate heart. Because she was coping with her daughter's seizures and a major concussion, Rose understood my brain injury and disabilities. God clearly orchestrated our meeting, because Rose had recently moved to my area to be closer to her job, and I had just started attending her church.

Rose and I had a very romantic engagement six months after we met and were married six months later. Rose's daughters openly embraced me, helping to ease the pain of losing my relationship with my own daughters.

God answered my prayer for a family. He provided me with a loving Christian wife, three fun-loving daughters, a son-in-law, and two adorable grandchildren—all who accept me as I am. I couldn't be happier! We continue to pray for my daughters and know that one day they will return to us because God has been so faithful to answer our prayers!

The angel from the hospital room told me I would get better. Although I have made significant improvements physically, my emotional and spiritual growth has been enormous. I not only came to know Christ, but have been able to experience the strength He provides.

One Sunday, Rose and I were sitting in the cafeteria at church. My friend and former colleague Bill walked up to us.

He stared. "Ray, is that you? How long have you been coming here?" After hearing my story, tears trickled down his face.

"I have been praying for you for ten years! I placed a prayer stone with your name on it under the altar of this church! Praise God! He's answered my prayers!"

Breaking Selfish Pride

FAITH TURNET

Facing the threat of lawsuits, job termination, and a ruined reputation were the best things that ever happened to me.

I can utter those words with a peaceful heart now that I'm removed from the darkest journey of my personal and professional life, but it was a different story several years ago.

In April 2008, I was deeply engrossed in research and activities associated with a doctoral program to further enhance my profession as a public school educator. I had transitioned from classroom teacher to assistant principal and knew the next step in the journey was the coveted title of principal.

I had my professional career all mapped out to the point that I could envision grandiose titles under the United States Department of Education in my twilight years. In my mind, I was an educational powerhouse who could do no wrong.

But those grandiose dreams came to a screeching halt in the spring of 2008, when the family of a student in my school became dissatisfied. The complaints moved beyond "We just don't like her" to "She struck our child, as evidenced by this bruise!" The bruise on the child's back actually came from a tumble on the playground, but the accusation of abuse was out there.

As a Bible-believing woman and a dedicated teacher and administrator, I would never even consider striking a child. I treated students fairly, loved them, listened when they were distraught, and disciplined respectfully when they disobeyed. But *abuse?* The mention of that word sent shock waves through my system.

A police investigator visited me at school with a long series of questions that drove my blood pressure through the roof. This interrogation was followed by phone calls with school district personnel and attorneys.

The family, besides requesting my dismissal from the school, also threatened to sue me. I was facing criminal charges, lawsuits, and termination at the ripe old age of thirty-five. With no history of legal concerns, I now faced the worst complaint possible.

During this painful season, I couldn't sleep, eat, think, or speak. I could only cry while friends or family members held me. My broken dreams, hopes, and reputation overwhelmed me to the point that I felt life really wasn't worth living. All I could do was cry and pray. Many days my prayers were wordless. My agony was so intense that I could only ask God to hold me, love me, and somehow protect me through this horrible storm.

Like Jonah, I wanted to be thrown overboard. I wanted to disappear into the deep waters of confusion and despair and hope that everything was just a really bad nightmare. After all, how could a loving and faithful God allow a good little Baptist girl like me to face such a frightening experience?

Some days I felt like a persecuted Job who never asked for the hardship. Other days, I felt akin to a laughing, skeptical Sarah who doubted God's ability to do the impossible.

After weeks of investigative work, the good news came that the police saw no evidence of wrongdoing and would not charge me with a crime. Relief. Pure, joyful relief! But this was only the calm before the storm.

Within twenty-four hours, I was summoned to the school district headquarters where I heard, "We don't think you can cut it anymore. You're not meeting our expectations. We're disappointed in you."

In the blink of an eye, I faced a decision I thought I would never have to face: Walk away from the job that I loved deeply and leave public education, or take a new job within the system as a writer until my contract expired. Option two was a professional demotion, but demotion seemed preferable to unemployment.

How would I explain to all of my colleagues and doctoral program friends why I was no longer in my dream job? How could someone working to obtain the highest degree possible explain that she was no longer "good enough" for this job? And how could I now report to a boss who looked me in the eye and told me I just wasn't cutting it? How could I endure this change?

The anger, frustration, and pain I felt when I had to kiss all of my professional dreams good-bye and with Christian kindness say, "Sure, I'll gladly make a professional change. I'll take the demotion and subsequent pay reduction. I'll hold my head high and do a good job," is indescribable.

I made it out of the office and as far as the driver's seat of my car before I collapsed into a fit of fears and tears.

The days that followed the threats of lawsuits, termination, and a deeply bruised ego are a blur at this point, but they are days that I survived because of the power of a lot of prayer, and not just my own. I had been blessed with a devout mother, father, sister, extended family, and church members who believed that prayer held power. When I couldn't pray, they interceded for me. They went to their knees daily for me, asking God to make something beautiful out of this mess of my broken life.

In those dark days, it was powerful, on-your-knees kind of prayer that turned a charge of child abuse into a dismissal, a lawsuit into dropped litigation, and a termination into a testimony of God's provision for my life.

The new, demoted position to support district writing efforts actually offered me the opportunity to engage in rigorous research and writing for educational purposes. With less stress and better hours I could concentrate on finishing my doctoral degree and finding balance in life, even though the paycheck and job title were less impressive. Furthermore, the new position allowed me to develop stronger writing, editing, and data analysis skills, skills that serve me well today.

After four years as a writer, I was able to join an international education company. The demotion that I thought ended my professional success was God's first building block for future financial blessing and professional satisfaction.

But more important, the painful journey was God's plan at its finest—the first stepping-stone toward becoming a deeper, devout, radically changed believer who finally grasped the power and purpose of prayer.

During this season I came to a new understanding of Jesus during the final hours of His life. Mark 14:35 says Jesus "fell to the ground and prayed."

Many of us gloss over this part of the crucifixion and resurrection story to get to the "really good part" about the angel and the stone. But the "good part" actually starts in that garden of Gethsemane, when Jesus fell to the ground in passionate, purposeful prayer. His season of prayer helped prepare Him for the most agonizing season of life. Prayer helped Him face the ultimate betrayal with grace, dignity, strength, and compassion. Prayer prepared Jesus for the unthinkable.

My painful, life-altering season was nothing compared to what Jesus faced, but like the Savior, I found that my only option, the best option, in the face of false charges and lies was to fall before my Daddy God, asking for strength to put one foot in front of the other.

Although the best part of my story may appear to be how God saved me from false charges of child abuse, permanent termination, and a frightening lawsuit, I learned in time that the best part of the story was the breaking of my selfish pride. Before this journey, I was so wrapped up in myself, my skills, and my experiences that I hadn't taken time to invite God into my life. God only factored in when I was the most desperate.

These circumstances forced me to look at the woman in the mirror and to question whether, like Jesus, I was praying, "Not my will, but thine be done," or attempting to be the author of my own story.

The greatest testimony of my journey is that God not only did the impossible with my circumstances but also with me.

The Final Authority

ELFRIEDE VOLK

In the spring of 1946, the war was over, but in our little city of Freiburg, now Swiebodzice, a battle was still raging, garnering more casualties than the war had. With immune systems compromised by malnutrition and starvation, people were falling victim to diseases brought on by lack of hygiene, parasites, and polluted water. As no medical help was available, the result was a typhus epidemic that seemed to be unstoppable.

"If you get sick," people whispered to each other, "don't go to the hospital. The Russians will just inject you with some air, and when the bubble gets to the heart, it's over. One less German to worry about, as far as they're concerned."

We were not Germans. My father, the son of a Dutch fisherman, had come to Germany years earlier to find employment to help his family when pollution decimated the fish in the Frisian Lakes. True to his Frisian heritage, Dad stubbornly persisted where others would have given up long ago, and eventually he was successful. He was also devout and unfailing in his belief in God. He prayed before and after each meal, and insisted that God's Word should be part of his daily bread.

In Germany, he met some Christians who worshiped on Saturday. Even as a boy, he had wondered why people went to church on the first day of the week when the Bible said that the seventh was the Sabbath, so he gladly worshiped with them. Falling in love, he married and settled in Germany, where we children were born.

When the Depression left many people unemployed, Dad embarked on a new venture, starting a business selling fish and fresh fruits and vegetables. After all, food is one of the most basic needs of life, and always in demand. But the war ended this business because he was unable to obtain fuel to make his deliveries.

He was also unable to take his family back to his homeland. So to avoid being conscripted into the Organisation Todt, he volunteered with the Red Cross and worked in a hospital until the war ended. When armistice came, we were under Russian and Polish occupation and in the midst of a raging typhus epidemic.

Aware of the dangers of allowing infectious diseases to run rampant, Dad contacted the Russian occupation forces to offer his help. Since he had a horse and wagon, he was ordered to go from house to house each day to pick up the bodies of those who had succumbed to typhus overnight and to take them out of town for mass burial.

Before he left, he gave us strict instructions: "Boil some water and use it to scrub your hair thoroughly with lye soap. Then comb your hair with a fine-tooth comb to dislodge any lice and their eggs. Don't drink water from the tap. Don't even use it to wash food or your hands. Boil it thoroughly first. Even boil the dishes you eat from. And pray. Don't forget to pray that God will keep you from getting sick, too."

Despite all precautions, my sister Ruth, thirteen years old, came down with typhus. Toward the end of the war, the school had been bombed, so there were no classes. Neither was there food. Some neighbors were eating rats and mice to keep alive, while one killed his entire family before taking his own life, as he could not bear to see them starve.

Since store shelves were empty, Ruth had gone into the country to forage for edibles. She had become thirsty. Though she had a bottle of boiled water with her, the cool, sparkling water in a roadside stream proved irresistible, and she drank. After all, she thought, it was not from the tap, and she didn't realize that the effluent from decaying bodies had leached into the groundwater.

Whether due to the water or too close contact with friends, a few days later she developed a cough, a splitting headache, and high fever. She lapsed into unconsciousness, and someone carried her home.

Mother immediately isolated Ruth in one of our two rooms, and she wore a mask and long gown whenever she tended to Ruth, hanging these on a hook by the doorframe when she came out. She also set up a washstand at the door, where she washed her hands before going into Ruth's room and after coming out. Any linens or towels used for Ruth were boiled, as well as her dishes, which were boiled separately from ours.

The disease lingered for days. Each day, Mother spent more time with Ruth, and each day her eyes seemed to be more sunken in her worn face. At first, Mother had sung to Ruth, but after a few days her songs ceased. So did her smiles. They were replaced by a haggard, almost hopeless expression.

When they had not seen Ruth for several weeks, neighbors became suspicious, and then alarmed. They demanded that Dad take her to a hospital so that she would not infect others.

"She gets much better care here," Dad said. "But if you are worried that you might catch something, we'll keep the other children inside, too."

That was not good enough for one person, who lodged a complaint with the Russian authorities. Two officers came, did an inspection, and left again.

"We can't do more than what you are already doing here," they said. "Keep up the good work. And if anyone else complains, refer them to us."

After they had gone, we sent up a prayer of thanks. At home, Ruth had constant and undivided attention, whereas in the overcrowded hospital she would be but one patient among many.

As the disease continued and Ruth showed no signs of improvement, Dad's face also reflected his concern. His prayers became longer and more frequent, more earnest. He often relieved Mother at Ruth's bedside, passing long, sleepless hours in prayer.

Intestinal disturbances are part of the disease, and there was constantly a large kettle of linens boiling on the stove. Millie, two years older than Ruth, was responsible to do the laundry and hang clothes to dry. With widespread theft and pillaging, we could no longer hang clothes outside, so Millie carried the wet items up to the attic.

Crying, I followed her wherever she went. At four, I could not understand what was happening. I just knew that I was hungry, that I hurt, and that I missed Ruth and my mother.

Since Mother had not been well even before I was born, Ruth had been the one who usually looked after me.

A few days later, I saw Mother crying, too. She ran out of Ruth's room, and didn't even stop to wash her hands or hang up her gown. "Ruth is dead. Ruth is dead," she wailed as she collapsed into Dad's arms.

Dad looked shocked. Then a determined expression settled on his face.

"I don't believe it," he said. "I *won't* believe it!"

Turning to us children, he said, "Come into Ruth's room. And Mother, bring me some oil."

I could not recognize Ruth when I saw her. Her beautiful blond hair had fallen out and she was bald. Her once-rosy cheeks were white, the skin draped in folds over the bony structure underneath. Her eyes were closed and sunken into their sockets.

"She is not dead," Dad said, gently laying her bony hand back on the covers. "She is only in a coma. But the Bible gives us instructions on what to do when someone is sick. God can still help, even when the situation appears hopeless."

He opened his Bible to James 5:14–15 and read, *"Is anyone among you sick? Let them call the elders of the church to pray over them and anoint them with oil in the name of the Lord. And the prayer offered in faith will make the sick person well; the Lord will raise them up. If they have sinned, they will be forgiven."*

"As our church members were scattered during the war, we have no elders to call on," Dad continued. "But we do have each other, and as a family we can pray for Ruth. As I was a church elder, I can anoint her. And while I am doing that and praying, I want each of you to pray, too. Remember what the Bible says: 'The prayer offered in faith will make the sick person well.' We need to take God at His Word and believe what He says."

I knelt down with Millie and my brothers at the foot of Ruth's bed while Dad and Mother were at the head. I had been taught to close my eyes for prayer, but I confess that this time I peeked. I wanted to see what God would do. I believed with all my heart. I knew I wouldn't be able to see Him, but I also knew He would do *something.*

God did not heal her immediately, but the fever left her. In the next few days, her rash faded and her intestinal disturbances settled down. She was able to open her eyes and speak. With help, she was even able to sit up. Before too long she was feeling hungry and eating again. And Mother was singing and smiling again.

Slowly, Ruth regained the use of her muscles and limbs. When she held her arms up, the skin draped from them like limp rags.

"Look at what I can do," she said, smiling wanly. "I can push my finger between the bones of my arms. When I fatten up again, I won't be able to do that anymore."

The first time Ruth ventured onto the street, people ran away screaming. "What's wrong with them?" she asked. "They act as if they've seen a ghost!"

"Not a ghost," Millie laughed. "But you must admit that you look like a skeleton."

Through the Red Cross, we were taken to a refugee camp in Sweden not long afterward, and for the first time in years were able to fill our stomachs. With wholesome food, Ruth regained her health and strength and her hair grew in again. When we all were able to pass our medical exams, we were repatriated to the Netherlands, from where we immigrated to Canada. Here

Ruth met and fell in love with a young man who had also been displaced by the war.

"I'm sorry," the doctor told her when he did her prenuptial medical exam. "With what you have gone through, and with the seriousness of the typhus you suffered, you will never be able to have children."

Fortunately, God, and not doctors, is the final authority. And when God heals someone, He doesn't do it halfway. Ruth gave birth to five children and has numerous grandchildren. Now eighty-three, she never tires of telling people what God has done for her.

Home Is Where the Heart Is

James Stuart Bell

The idea of owning our own home seemed like a distant dream, and initially I didn't think that there was any hurry. I had been a graduate student in Ireland, and my Irish wife, Margaret, got pregnant right away. We came back to the States and briefly lived with my parents as I looked for some type of writing or communications job. I found a low-paying job through a government grant with the American Heart Association as their public relations person.

After our adorable baby Rosheen was born, it was time to move out of my parents' beautiful home in a posh suburb and find a humble place of our own.

I had high expectations, but very little money. Margaret was happy to simply find a place within our meager budget and begin the nesting process. We settled on a small one-bedroom apartment that was cozy enough for the three of us. But as time went by, we were expecting another baby and wondering how that would work with an apartment that had a postage-stamp-size kitchen, a bathroom that seemed about the size of a phone booth, and a bedroom that resembled an oversized walk-in closet.

Our apartment was on the second floor and had a stairway down to the entrance. We put up a gate to prevent our daughter from falling down the stairs. But it only took one moment of forgetfulness, and I watched in horror as she spilled down the stairs, feet entangled in her walker.

Plus, the neighborhood residents were having their own struggles a bit too close to home. The guy whose window we could look directly into from ours stuck his head in an oven after an altercation with his girlfriend. I could hear it unfold. It was time to consider moving.

Then it happened. My parents were casually looking around for something larger to encompass our growing family. They landed on what seemed to be a bonanza—a brand-new housing development was going up with reasonable prices. I smiled as I thought about my own little plot of land and no cockroaches in the kitchen.

All of us took off on the weekend to see this smallish colonial. In my mind, nothing is quite like the excitement of new construction and watching homes going up with all new neighbors. I had experienced this three times in my own childhood when my parents built brand-new homes.

As we asked the realtor questions and toured the home, I felt like it was too good to be true. The finances just barely worked, but this was in a time when home values were escalating and, according to my parents, it would be a good investment. The only downside appeared to be a dilapidated barn with a couple of old wrecked cars right behind what would be our backyard.

Views and trees really appeal to me, but I thought I shouldn't expect too much and be content with this superb gift. Then, just as we were ready to leave, Rosheen fell down the stairs of the new home. We had been praying fervently for confirmation on our way to the house. Was this a negative sign?

When we came back to our little mole hole, we continued to pray. As a typical man, I was listing the facts, confident that my bride would see common sense and would also love a bigger home to take care of and decorate. But to my chagrin, she blurted out that she didn't have peace about it from the Lord. I was a bit shocked and asked her reasons. She said she had none but the intuitive check that we can sometimes get from the Holy Spirit. To my credit, I had to check my heart and seek out my own motivations before trying to pressure her with facts. What could possibly be wrong with a home that we could afford and that would be a good investment, especially with the prediction that mortgage interest rates would continue to go up?

Fortunately, I had learned a good bit from marriage conferences, books, and some other couples married longer than we were at the time. If you have a godly wife and after prayer on a certain issue you don't have peace or you are not in agreement, then don't move forward. She wouldn't budge because she didn't want to violate what she sensed the Lord was telling her. It was clear that we were being tested. It wasn't necessarily wrong to buy this house, but would we be willing to obey God for what He ultimately had planned for us? So we made the decision to pass it up, and we could find nothing else like it on the market.

Over the ensuing couple of years, interest rates did indeed climb, but so did my salary with a new high-profile job in New York City, and we were able to increase our savings. Our apartment began to feel like a sardine can when our son Brendan arrived, and then later a relative with her new baby for six months, to make a total of six sardines! But God was teaching us about sharing with others, learning to live on less, and putting Him above earthly desires. In fact, we put the goal of a new house completely out of our minds, and asked God, when He was ready, to just give us a sign to pursue a change in our living situation.

One of our clients in a nearby tree-lined and more rural suburb had me come out for a visit. On my way back, I passed a sign saying NEW HOUSES FOR SALE. I cruised down the street, passing houses being constructed, to a dead end where there was an empty lot. As I surveyed the beautiful woods on three sides, I wondered why this lot was one of the last available and wished the fortunate person well. On my way out, I stopped off at the builder's model home. He conveyed to me that the reason the lot was available was that the original owner's financing had fallen through at the last moment. What was really interesting was that this builder was the same one who built the home we had decided not to buy two years earlier because of our discernment in prayer.

I drove home at the speed of light and grabbed a hold of Margaret; we drove back to talk to the builder in greater detail. It turns out that he could put the exact same model that we had previously turned down on this prime lot. It would take him six months to build, and because of my improved salary, we could save more for a down payment on what had become a slightly more expensive home. We had the additional perk, with new construction, of weekly watching our home ascend to the sky. And because of the location, we didn't have to forego the joy of the trees or deal with the eyesore of rusted-out cars behind our backyard.

It was as if God introduced what was ideal for us at the time but was testing our hearts in terms of not getting ahead of His will. After we moved in, we realized that because of the cul-de-sac and no house across the street, our young children were able to play in the street in front of our yard without worry. Not so at the previous house two miles away. We were able to walk behind our backyard and follow a long path between the trees in solitude when we wanted to pray or think through a decision. Not so, again, with the first home two years previous.

Whenever we think back thirty-five years upon the joy of entering that house after waiting so long, and all the wonderful memories that ensued with our children, we ask ourselves: "Would we rather have lived in the first house with its downsides for eleven years? Or waited as we did for the additional blessings and the nine years we had at the second house?" The answer is always the same, and we praise God all over again for the house at 30 Pierson Drive.

Home is indeed where the heart is, and we'll find it by seeking the Lord's will and timetable and making sure He is first in our hearts.

No More Headaches

MARTY PRUDHOMME

At seven years of age, I began suffering with headaches. My Mom called them sick headaches because I would throw up. We had not heard the term *migraine*. Many holidays, picnics, and other family functions were ruined because I was ill.

My parents thought it was because I became overly excited, and the stress would bring on a headache. They often admonished, "Now, don't get too excited, but we are going on a picnic next week. You will be all right if you stay calm."

Their well-intended suggestions did not help.

We did not have money for doctors, except in extreme circumstances. Once while I was playing with my brother, he fell and broke his arm. Now, that warranted a trip to the doctor, but headaches did not. My parents prayed that I would outgrow my inconvenient illness.

The headaches eventually tapered off, and by high school they were completely gone—although my parents began having headaches dealing with a typical teenager!

In college, I met Bill, who was to become my husband. He was a tall, very good-looking fellow. After we married, Bill's job required us to move to Virginia. I suddenly began to suffer with sinus headaches. Whenever the weather turned nice, the headaches would start. The beautiful fall days were the worst, but at least I was not throwing up anymore.

Eventually, Bill found a job in Louisiana. We thought I would be free from the sinus allergies, but the headaches continued. I would tease Bill that I was allergic to him, since the headaches started up again after we were married. He did not think that was funny.

We soon had two children, and the cares of life piled up around us. Our marriage felt the stress and started to break apart. All I ever wanted in life was to be a wife and mom. I would shout at Bill, "You never want to spend time with me; all you do is work!"

That did not go over very well, and Bill would yell back, "You are such a nag! No wonder I don't want to spend time with you."

Our marriage problems caused me to cry out to God. After seeking God for answers, I was invited to a prayer group by some wonderful Christian women. They often prayed with me and taught me what the Bible had to say about my circumstances. After accepting the Lord into my life, I asked Him to take charge. I knew God could do a better job of running things than I had. I surrendered my life, my children, and even Bill to the Lord. Slowly things began to change; God took the anger in my heart and replaced it with His love.

Bill noticed the yelling diminished. He told me, "You should spend more time with those women; they are good for you."

Bill started going to a Christian men's group called the Full Gospel Business Men's Fellowship. He gave his life to the Lord, and we began to hope that God could bring real change to our marriage.

I invited a friend to come and teach a Bible study in our home. God was at work in us, but my headaches persisted—they occurred every time we met for Bible study. The horrible nausea came back, but I would not cancel the study. The ladies prayed for me each week.

Doctors didn't have any answers. Pain pills gave me horrible side effects. I knew prayer was the only answer, even as the frequency of the headaches increased to several days a week.

Once I was to sing for a friend's wedding, but when the day arrived I awoke in extreme pain. I was so nauseated I lay on the bathroom floor with my cheek on the cool tile. If I moved, the retching would begin. I was concerned that no one could take my place for the wedding. My friends would be terribly disappointed if there was no soloist for the ceremony.

Bill called Brenda to come and pray for me. Brenda was my teacher and mentor who taught me the importance of prayer when I first came to the Lord. She prayed, "In the name of Jesus, headache go and nausea stop. We claim the healing that was paid for on Calvary."

Nothing special happened, but I soon realized the pain and nausea were gone. That afternoon I was able to get dressed and made it to the wedding. I rejoiced in the Lord my healer.

I thought I was totally healed, but when the Bible study came around that week, so did the headache.

As we joined hands, the Lord's presence was so sweet. The ladies' prayers warmed and comforted me. Jesus was my healer, no matter my circumstances. I would often lie on the bathroom floor, praying, "Jesus, if you never heal me, I will praise you anyway, for you are worthy. As long as I have breath I will praise you, O Lord."

I was very concerned for my children during this season. They were in school and still needed Mama to get them off to classes, to help with homework, and to cook their dinner. They needed me to tuck them into bed and say good-night prayers. Some days it was impossible to give them the attention they needed, and I felt guilty. My friends' prayers sustained me as I continued to trust the Lord.

One day, Brenda phoned and invited Bill and me to go with her and her husband to hear evangelist T.L. Osborn speak. He had a powerful healing ministry in Africa and was traveling around the United States.

The evangelist shared many miraculous stories about what God was doing. He and his wife, Daisy, had seen thousands come to know Christ during their crusades. T.L. told us, "Jesus taught His disciples what normal Christianity was like. The gospel is to be preached everywhere, the sick healed, and the oppressed set free. God desires that His ministry be part of our everyday lives if we will only believe."

At the end of the service T.L. said, "This crowd is too large for everyone to come forward for prayer. I would like everyone who needs healing to place your hands where it hurts." He prayed, "Dear Lord, you see the needs and know every sickness in this room. In the name of Jesus, I ask for all sickness to leave—let all disease and all pain be gone."

His prayer was not lengthy, but I knew the Lord heard his prayer and all the prayers that had been offered over the past years on my behalf. I didn't have goose bumps or any warmth, as some say they feel when God has healed them. I didn't feel anything at all except a small pop in my ears.

As we left the church that night, I hesitated to say anything to my friends, because it was such a small sensation in my ears. When we got into the car, I thought, *By faith, I'm going to tell them I felt a pop in my ears, and I believe God has healed me.*

They did not seem very excited about my comment, but talked about how the Osborns' testimonies had encouraged them. I silently thanked the Lord for His healing.

These events took place more than thirty years ago. Since that day, I have not had a single headache. No more sinus headaches when the weather changes, no headaches when I get hungry or when I'm under stress, and definitely no migraines. The Lord heard all those prayers, over the years, and when the time was right, He answered. God miraculously healed me.

God exhorts us to pray, and then He answers our prayers. Even if the answers are delayed, God is faithful. Never, ever give up. Never stop praying. Praise the Lord, for He is a God who hears and answers prayer.

Father Knows Best

Dorothy J. Haire

A group of giggly twelve-year-old girls sat on the iron rail fence of the local elementary school, watching skinny boys play basketball. Suddenly, one boy broke away from the crowd and dribbled the ball to me. With his thirteen-and-a-half-year-old changing voice he announced for all to hear, "I love you!" and dribbled back to the other boys.

The girls giggled, and the boys cheered! Refusing to admit I heard him, I continued to talk to the girl sitting next to me. I was twelve, and had no interest in boys in general, and now him in particular, since he had humiliated me in front of everyone. I never wanted to see him again.

I later found out that his name was Johnnie Lee Haire. For the next two years, he stalked me. He was everywhere: school dances, basketball games, walking home from school, always proclaiming his love.

By the time I was fourteen, my mother allowed him to come over and sit on the porch for a while. She loved his "Yes, Ma'am," "No, Ma'am," "Thank you," and "Can I pick that up for you, Ms. Bessie?"

Two weeks before my seventeenth birthday, I married that boy—my best friend and soul mate. Thirty-three years and four adult children later, we were making plans as new empty nesters to live our wildest dreams. We were so happy.

I could not imagine life without Johnnie. I was confident I would never have to live without him, because I had talked with God about it. Johnnie's possible death had become a concern for me when my friend Dee's husband suddenly passed away. They were such a loving couple. One night they went to sleep; she woke up the next morning, but he did not. I was in shock. This was unbelievable. I went to their house to see for myself if this was true. The look on Dee's face said it all. I never wanted to experience that kind of pain.

I knew John 14:13–14: "Whatever you ask in My name, that I will do, so that the Father may be glorified in the Son. If you ask Me anything in My name, I will do it" (NASB).

I prayed all the way home, pleading with Jesus to take me home first. I explained to Him that I was an only child and all alone, except for Johnnie and our four children. Mama had passed years before. Johnnie had brothers and sisters who would help him finish raising our children. I told Jesus that I could not live without Johnnie—my friend, my lover, my soul mate, my everything.

When I got home, I sat Johnnie down at the kitchen table. I explained what had happened to Dee. I repeated to him my prayer to God. I made him promise he would not die before me. Confident that God and Johnnie understood the desires of my heart and agreed, I went on with my life.

A couple of years later, while we were laughing and talking, Johnnie began to cough. Then he began to hyperventilate.

"You caught a cold?" I asked as I passed him a brown paper bag to breathe into, which slowed his breathing.

"No, I don't have a cold."

"Lie down and rest. You'll feel better." I went to the family room to read so I would not disturb him.

"Hey, Mama, y'all got something to eat?" our son Tommie asked as he came in the front door headed to the kitchen. A few minutes later, we both heard labored breathing. Running into the bedroom, we realized Johnnie was in trouble.

"You are going to the hospital," I informed Johnnie while motioning for Tommie to help me get him dressed. We walked him through the house to the front door.

"What is this, Dorothy?" he struggled to ask.

"I don't know, but I know Jesus does," I answered. As I prayed, Tommie and I began walking his rapidly weakening body to the car to take him to the emergency room. He collapsed onto the back seat of the car. We arrived at the hospital in ten minutes, horn blasting all the way.

The police at the hospital entrance must have radioed ahead because the ER staff burst out of the door with a gurney as we pulled up. They whisked him away, directing us to the waiting room. A few minutes later, the doctor came out to tell us that Johnnie had died of a massive heart attack.

There was no warning and no pain. He was not sick in any way. The love of my life, my soul mate, my best friend was gone!

Standing beside Johnnie's bed with my hand on his still-warm chest, I heard a loud voice say, *"Nothing left undone. Nothing left unsaid. No regrets."*

The authority and love in this voice prevented feelings of sorrow, anger, and betrayal from entering my heart. Peace filled me and encapsulated me.

Standing beside the bed of my childhood sweetheart in the emergency room, the unthinkable happened. I was happy for him. After all, isn't that what all saints want—to finish their course in a way that pleases God? No pain. No time to fret. Just a call to come home, and it was over. Johnnie was with Jesus, and I was happy for him.

But what about me?

I prayed, "Jesus, help me through the next hour."

He did.

I repeated that prayer for a few days until it evolved to "Jesus, help me through this day."

He did.

Gradually I started to pray, "Jesus, help me through this week."

He did.

I thought I could not live without Johnnie, and if I did I would be dysfunctional. It was not true. After the funeral was over and all my friends returned to their lives, God proved himself to be more than enough for me. Daily He stabilizes my heart with His love, which makes me strong. I feel God's presence every day, which gives me peace. I pray for guidance before going to sleep and awake with the answers to my problems.

Johnnie was a good provider. I also worked, and together we were able to provide vacations, a comfortable home, college educations, and nice clothes for our children.

God became an extravagant provider, not only taking care of my daily needs but also making my dreams come true. I had always wanted to travel abroad. So far I have been to London, Paris, Rome, Egypt, and Israel.

It was Johnnie's time to go home and be with the Lord. Now that it has happened, I am okay with it. My adult children have homes, children, and lives of their own; but I am not alone, nor lonely. Also, I have a new heart's desire. I want God to be able to say about me the words He spoke about Johnnie: *"Nothing left undone. Nothing left unsaid. No regrets."* My goal every day is to live in such a way that God would be pleased with me.

Often we think we are praying about one thing, when really we are praying about something else. My prayer was not motivated by love for Johnnie, but my unwillingness to live without him. God listens past the words of our mouths and hears the words of our hearts. In His infinite wisdom, He answers the prayers of our hearts in ways we could not fathom with our finite minds. I am so very grateful that our Father knows best.

Shortest, Biggest Prayer

CHARLES J. HUFF

I heard an engine growl as the driver stomped on the gas pedal. I gave no thought to it until I heard the harrowing squall of brakes. I looked up and saw my five-year-old daughter, Nicole, in the middle of the street, staring wild-eyed at the approaching car careening toward her.

A friend of mine and I were working on a car across the street from our house. Nicole, wanting to be a part of what was happening, was watching everything we did.

The hood was up. I was sitting in the driver's seat as my friend worked on the engine. He said he needed another tool and headed for my garage. When he reached the edge of my yard, Nicole decided to chase after him.

Everything that happened and all that went through my mind in the next three seconds made time seem to stretch into minutes. I looked in the door mirror and caught the image of the bumper moving forward then out of view. Turning to look out the window, I saw the fear in the eyes of the driver and his passenger.

Time stopped to allow me to recall a friend's story about a miracle involving his young grandson—a miracle that started as a horrible tragedy. He told how the preschooler had been struck by a car. Instead of being knocked to the side, clear of the car, he was knocked down and the car passed over him, stopping with the muffler resting on top of him. His grandson's flesh was seared and stuck to the muffler. Medics had to tear part of his skin off in order free him.

Through his tears, my friend gave glory to Jesus, saying that the boy not only lived but also had almost no scarring.

The thought of my beautiful little girl experiencing the same fate clawed at my soul. With the car passing beside me, I couldn't jump out and grab her or push her out of the way. This was one time all I could do was pray, but I didn't have time to tell Jesus all my fears. I didn't have time to tell Him how much I wanted Him to keep her from falling beneath the car.

Tires were still screeching, and the car continued to bear down on my little girl. The closer the car got to her, the more my heart collapsed.

I only had time to cry out, "Jesus!"

That one-word prayer contained everything I wanted to say to Him. He knows the thoughts of our hearts even before we speak them. I know this because she flew up into the air, not under the car, and the car continued skidding forward, moving underneath her. "Thank you, Jesus."

I saw her falling toward the car's windshield with the car still moving forward. A memory from my youth flashed in my mind—a young cousin of mine was struck by a car while he was riding his bicycle. He flew up and crashed down through the windshield, lost half of his face, and died of head trauma.

Again, I cried out, "Jesus!"

In that one-word prayer, I asked the Lord to prevent her from going through the windshield. With the car's forward movement, she hit the car just above the windshield. The impact caused her to fly forward where she then grazed the front edge of the hood as the driver fought to stop the car. I again thanked the Lord for hearing and answering my prayer.

I had prayed against two immediate hazards, but now I realized other disastrous possibilities. What if she landed on her head? She could be killed, receive a concussion, or break her neck. She could already have broken bones and break more.

The car still had not stopped, so the fear of it moving on top of her speared me once more. For the third time, I cried out, "Jesus!"

I can still see her little body, arms and legs flailing wildly like a rag doll tossed into the air. However, just as vivid in my mind is how her body turned after glancing off the hood so she rolled like a pencil in front of the now stopped car. At last I was able to get out of the car and run to her.

I made her lie still in spite of her cries to get off the hot pavement. I prayed over her as we waited for an ambulance.

The driver kept apologizing, in his attempt to convince me he could have done nothing to prevent this. I told him I knew Jesus had already answered many prayers for her and that I believed she would be fine.

The ambulance came and took her to the hospital. The emergency room personnel confirmed God's protective power. She had only a couple of minor scrapes and bruises. I sent the driver the news from the hospital so he could know how great our God is.

We are so thankful to the Lord for all that He did for us in that accident. We thank Him and praise Him, too, for the lesson on prayer. Before the accident, our family had read and talked about King David's crying out to the Lord.

In Psalm 3, David wrote, "I cried to the Lord with my voice, and He heard me from His holy hill" (v. 4 NKJV). The heading to this psalm informs us David wrote it when he fled from his own son Absalom. David, God's own anointed. David, the King of Israel. David, the man after God's own heart. David, who slew Goliath, and the one of whom all of Israel sang, "Saul has slain his thousands, and David his tens of thousands" (1 Samuel 18:7).

This same David cried out to the Lord in desperation and taught us a valuable lesson on prayer. How long does a prayer have to be in order to be effective? How much detail do we need to express, or how many specifics do we need to give Him in our prayers?

According to David's example, not one of these questions or concerns really matters, since God knows what is in our hearts already. Like David, I cried out to the Lord with my voice, and He heard me, and He answered me.

A Race to the Bottom

SUSAN M. WATKINS

W hen you're a tenured Christian, you've heard about multiple venues for answered prayers. God is indeed resourceful, and like the flow of water, He effortlessly gets into the smallest cracks. He's never limited by calendars, geography, or hemispheres. Past, present, and future pose no boundaries. He doesn't need cars, airplanes, passports, or birth certificates. He truly is everywhere, and He truly does know all of our days before we reach them.

Some fifteen years before I uttered my prayer, God initiated His answer. He's like that. Isaiah wrote that God hears before we speak; answers before we ask (Isaiah 65:24).

Young and energetic, and having recently moved to Arizona from a big city, I was always up for new challenges.

Quick to organize anything, the task often fell to me to plan something fun and exciting, so one cool morning while doves cooed, perched atop abundant cacti, several of us loaded into cars to embark on a day of mountain climbing. The day promised to be blistering hot, so we had to start early to get ahead of the heat. Despite our early start, the sun was fully awake and the car's air conditioner ran at maximum output. Altitude popped our ears as we wound up the mountain's two-lane paved road. This peak's elevation reached 9,200 feet. Boulders often littered the roadway and had shattered the pavement upon impact. Between the ponderosa pines we passed, we could see the city basin below with heat waves already dancing above it. Our engine's strain eased when we reached a cool enough altitude that we could turn off the air conditioning and lower the windows. The mountain's fragrance filled the vehicle. I longed to stretch my legs as I thought about my childhood filled with riding trains, buses, taxis, and subways. The city idea of a "trail ride" was to let kids ride saddled horses on streets alongside rush-hour traffic. My new environment surprisingly suited me, and I was open to all possibilities.

This mountain range was becoming familiar to me. I'd already hiked it a few times, but this outing promised a higher trail. On the mountain's opposite side was a rugged cave for truly adventurous spelunking. It was not the destination for people who were unwilling to crawl in the mud on their bellies through extremely tight spaces. Within days of learning about it, I was facedown in the mud, scraping my back along jagged rock formations. I exited the cave twenty pounds heavier from caked-on mud and was recognizable only by my voice. This caused several waiting novices to change their plans. Personally, I felt my greatest accomplishment wasn't exploring the intimidating cave, but not losing my hiking boots to the viscous mud and its insatiable appetite for all it touched.

Hours later, we reached our target. It looked rather ordinary instead of the classroom it was to become. I tell people that the view is always worth the climb, whether spiritually or naturally. Only by our commitment to the resistance will we reach the top. The climb delivers the reward.

As the group happily chatted, I scanned the area. We'd never climbed this high before, nearly at the ridge.

Early into the excursion, the terrain became much steeper than we expected and all but two less experienced climbers abandoned the journey. My friend and I pressed on well past the semblance of a trail until our passage narrowed sharply. Undeterred, we exited the tree line with unobstructed views of the glistening city. The altitude's beauty made me feel closer to God, not realizing how much I was about to need Him.

Our first dilemma was when we came to a ledge along the mountain's face that was only two feet wide, but widened again twenty-five feet ahead. Evaluating the discovery, we continued. The mountain above and below this ledge was sheer; however, the lower portion sloped somewhat and was covered completely in loose rocks.

My friend took the lead and told me to follow her footsteps. I did, but suddenly the ledge gave way and I slid down the mountainside. A lovely day of escaping the heat was now a life-threatening situation.

Because the surface beneath me was loose shale of various sizes, it actually increased my speed as I slid downward. The land surrounding this barren swath grew abundant pine trees, but not a stem or root grew where I was plummeting. It was a race to the bottom, and I already knew I wasn't going to win.

I'm always amazed at how people describe such situations as going in slow motion. I believe God wires us this way to give opportunity for solutions. I, too, had this experience. Only I used the long seconds to unleash the greatest power handed to humankind: Prayer.

All nineteen years of me asked the Almighty to be almighty. I had no chance of survival on my own. Even if I made it through whatever tragedy lay before me, I'd have a five-hour journey to a hospital. Being airlifted was unrealistic because I was literally on the side of a mountain. If the rocks didn't filet me after shredding my thin clothes, at some point something yet unseen *would* stop me.

No longer able to hear my friend's screams, I implored God to solve this physics problem. It wasn't the temporary prayer for deliverance with empty promises of lifetime service, but the sincere cries of a redeemed child to her heavenly Father, who'd granted another opportunity to prove himself faithful on her behalf.

As suddenly as I'd lost my footing and begun to pray, God did what God does best, and turned an earthly situation into a divine classroom.

Although I dug my heels into the shale, they failed to slow my ever-increasing speed. On my back, I continued scanning the surrounding landscape, hoping for something to grab. I prayed for any intervention to stop me.

I'd tried moving to the right and left, hoping it would create friction and reduce my speed. I crossed my arms and hands over my chest in an effort to protect them.

154

Desperately analyzing my situation, I finally visualized what was going to stop me. Jagged, sharp boulders formed a natural wall in all directions. They were impossible to avoid and a horrific collision lay just ahead. Unless God performed the miraculous, death was imminent, putting a definite wrinkle in my peace. I couldn't even fathom the pain upon impact.

Preparing for the worst, I suddenly saw a green dot enlarging as I approached and realized it was a plant that could rescue me. Some spring day, years earlier, God had caused a little windblown seed to take root on a mountainside, and despite rockslides and severe weather, it thrived until we met.

I began steering my speeding body toward the bush, hoping to crash into it instead of the boulders. With seconds left to maneuver into its path, I realized my "bush" was actually a wild prickly pear cactus covered with three-inch spike needles.

You've got to be kidding!

I rose up, slamming my entire body against the unconventional rescuer, grabbing it with all my remaining strength.

Then I screamed.

This was not Moses' burning bush, but I was delivered just the same. Had it been any other type of vegetation, it could not have survived on that mountainside. It had to be a tenacious cactus to endure its commission.

I came to a grinding halt and slowly peeled myself from that anchor. Crawling to the boulders just feet away, I discovered the road was on the other side, fifteen feet below. Had I survived the impact of smacking against the boulders, I'd have flipped over the steep embankment and potentially been run over by a car.

God answered numerous prayers that afternoon while He spared my life. Miraculously, my worst injuries were from cactus needles. The surface of the mountainside should have peeled me like a banana, broken several bones, and left me with severe internal injuries, but I sustained no injuries from sliding down the rocks, unprotected, at breakneck speed.

I learned our prayers are often answered in ways we're not expecting; however, He will *always* answer them.

Every single one of them—before we even ask.

Before the Snow Flies

LaRose Karr

Forging my car through deep, icy ruts was difficult and nerve-racking. It was unusual to have such a large amount of snow dumped on us this early in the season. Snow falls quickly in Colorado, and our city was not prepared to remove the heavy snow fast enough, so for three weeks, drivers barreled through unplowed snow, creating deep furrows of thick ice.

But sometimes you just have to brave the elements to do some shopping.

As I headed back home from my venture, suddenly I burst into laughter. The roads were just as bad as they'd been on my way into town, but instead of hunching over the steering wheel trying to deal with them, I unexpectedly exploded in glee.

I call this "holy laughter." It's when the joy of the Lord takes over and you laugh as you rejoice with Him. It's a simple pleasure, really, and just fun. Of course, it is perfectly fine to have a good time with the Lord, taking joy in the work of His hands.

And why were we rejoicing together?

The story began a year earlier in this same season of winter when I first heard the news: The structure of my long-time job was changing. Jobs do change at times, but I'd worked in this correctional setting for many years and had become burned out, as so many do from the stress and demands of a job.

With the new guidelines I would still put in forty hours a week at my regular job, my *home*, as it was called. But now everyone at my level were being asked to fill in for others as needed. For example, vacations, sick time, and training would take me to other areas in my workplace while employees were away from their desks or while empty positions were waiting to be filled.

This new policy may work well in small facilities, but I worked in a mega facility, spanning eighty acres, and the walking distance from the entrance to some areas was often a quarter of a mile.

I followed this new work plan for six months, and I became even more tired than I already was. I was well-equipped to handle one job, but adding in the distance between offices, differing work practices, policies, and people, and additional duties made me begin to feel stretched. Factor in heat and blizzards while walking to the various areas, and I had approached my limit. Walking in the early morning in extremely cold winter conditions exacerbated my bronchial problems.

As a severe asthmatic, I knew I needed to cut back on work, so I began to ask God for a part-time job that would allow me to work less and spend some time with my grandchildren. I also asked others I trusted to pray.

Instead of my load at work lightening, it increased. I was asked to leave my desk again, not only to perform the extra duties but also to begin working two afternoons a week in another area.

That's when I knew it was time to make a decision. My workload, not counting the filling in for other areas, had now increased from forty hours per week to forty-six. But I was not allowed to count overtime or accumulate compensation. All the work was to be accomplished in a regular workweek. As I pondered this problem and prayed about my desire to lighten my workload, I kept hearing the Lord's voice: *"Before the snow flies."*

What did He mean? Would I have a job by then? Was I supposed to leave my position before the snow flies?

Lord, what are you saying to me?

I started interviewing for other jobs, but nothing seemed appropriate or worked with the schedule I wanted, so I hung on to the job I had.

However, one morning I woke up sick, and I knew without a doubt that this was the day I was to give notice and watch for the employment doors the Lord was going to open for me. I just felt in my spirit that this was the day to speak. So I did.

Later that day, while reclining on the couch, not feeling well and covered with a blanket, I saw a newscast on television. Speaking of an area high in the Colorado mountains, the newscaster said, "Snow is flying in Colorado."

I laughed, thinking of that phrase the Lord had given me: *"Before the snow flies."*

My, how the Lord had arranged this event! I knew then that my obedience was needed before the snow fell. I had made my requests known to the Lord. He asked me to step out in faith and let go of my fears, and I had cut it to the wire.

After interviewing for three months, I was able to cut back as I wanted to for my health with a couple of part-time jobs. One came about right away with some work from home for a friend. Then another person offered me a job with the opportunity to work around the times I watched my grandchildren. Surprisingly, this marketing and social media employment came because of my computer knowledge and my calm voice. The business owner had even planned to fix up an office for me. I certainly never considered someone would create a job for me. There was no way my imagination could have dreamed of working with social media.

And six months earlier, when I had started petitioning the throne, how could I know that the job I would receive did not even exist yet? Perhaps the thought process of my future employer began at that time.

On this cold January day, I had driven the rutted, snowy streets of my town to shop. And as most small-town Americans know, local shopping is the social center for small towns. I came across two friends and told the story of how I acquired the jobs. One friend said, "I can see how this tickles you."

It did, indeed, tickle me. So as I drove home, I exploded with the joyous laughter of someone watching God's plans unfold precisely and completely, in God's way and in His timing.

Stepping out in faith for work provision is never easy, and because this was not the first time I had stepped out in faith, I already knew that the Lord knows the plans for us well in advance of our need. He is not surprised when we become burned out or tired. He has doors in place for us to step through, and while we are constrained by time, He is not.

Ask.

Seek.

Knock.

He will answer. Laughter and rejoicing are just around the corner.

Dad, Let's Pray!

BOBBIE ROPER

One of the scariest experiences of my life happened on a snowy November night in the Catskill Mountains of New York. My husband, Jim, had gone hunting that afternoon. Though many local guys hunted for sport or for trophy mounts, Jim hunted for the meat. Raising four children on a missionary's salary was not easy. A deer in the freezer went a long way to providing for our family.

Jim had been out several times over the past two weeks to no avail. Today was different. Just before dark, he'd shot a young buck with his compound bow. Quietly he eased out of the woods so the deer would lie down. After a couple of hours he would return, track it, bring it home, and prepare it for the freezer. Though he often did the tracking alone, on this night our twelve-year-old son, Jimmie, volunteered to help his dad. Not wanting to be left out, I decided to tag along.

We arrived at the spot where Jim had come out of the woods. We headed into the forest. I noticed right away that my nose hairs were freezing together as I breathed. Scattered patches of snow remained from a storm the week before, and the forecast called for heavy snow that night. The crunch of the frosty leaves reminded us how cold it was.

With thick cloud cover, our flashlights were our only source of light. I felt in the pocket of my heavy parka, making sure I had extra batteries. This cloudy night would not be a good time to run out of battery power.

Getting back to Jim's tree stand was fairly easy. He had glued squares of reflective tape to thumbtacks and placed a tack on every few trees at eye level. It amazed me how the tacks glowed when the light hit them. We found the tree where his stand was perched high above the ground. Now came the tough part—tracking the deer.

As we headed away from the tree stand, we could make out the trail of the buck through the heavy underbrush. A wounded deer always heads for the thickest cover, hoping to hide from whatever hurt it.

Eyes to the ground, ears alert for any sounds, Jim led the way. The deeper we went into the thick undergrowth, the harder it became. Blackberry vines ripped at our clothes, and in places we had to get on our hands and knees to make it through heavy underbrush.

As we pushed deeper, the temperature dropped. Snowflakes began drifting through the circle of light cast by Jimmie's flashlight. I asked Jim if we should turn around and head home.

"Just a little longer," he said. "That buck can't be too much farther."

After another ten minutes passed, we decided we would not find the deer. The snow was beginning to fall faster as the wind picked up. Even in this dense part of the woods the ground was becoming a white carpet. Pulling our hoods tighter, we headed back the way we thought we had come. We had been walking about fifteen minutes when Jim suddenly stopped.

"What's wrong?" I asked.

"We have walked in a circle," Jim said. "That's the same stump at the spot where we decided to turn back. But don't worry. I'll get us out of here."

Fifteen minutes later we still could not find the trail we had come in on. Snow had already covered the ground, making it impossible to see any signs of where we had been. The way Jimmie was walking told me that his feet were cold. His cheeks looked like candied apples and his lips were chapped. Why hadn't I grabbed my lip balm and a scarf for him?

Jim stopped, pulling us into his arms.

"Guys, I don't know how to get us out of here. It's hard to see with just our flashlights, and I left the compass in the truck. The temperature is dropping so fast, and between the wind and heavy snow I can't get my bearings. We will have to find a thicket to crawl into, and hopefully, if we stay close to each other we can keep warm enough to make it until morning. I am so sorry I let you come. I know you are scared. I just don't know what to do."

Sometimes as we raise our children we wonder if they are grasping anything we are trying to teach them. That night we learned that our son had indeed been listening. We had always taught our children the importance of walking close to God. We also taught them that our God is gracious and loving and answers our prayers. They had seen many prayers answered during the years when we were in Bible college and in our time as missionaries. So on this cold November night, when his dad was at a loss as to what to do, our son said in a shaky voice, "Dad, let's pray!"

This was an earnest plea from a child who believed that we faced a dilemma and that the God we worshiped would hear and answer. To him it was simple: We were in a fix and we needed to pray.

So there in the middle of the dark, ghostly woods, with the wind whistling through the trees and huge snowflakes falling around us, we knelt, joined hands, and lifted our faces heavenward.

"Lord," Jim prayed, "we need your help, and we could sure use it now. Show us the way out. We praise you for what you are going to do. Amen."

It was a simple prayer, but as the snowflakes melted on our faces, we felt a sense of peace. Surely the Lord was in this place. Jeremiah 33:3 came to mind: "Call to me and I will answer you and tell you great and unsearchable things you do not know." We were certainly trusting in that verse.

Only a couple of minutes later Jimmie shouted, "Dad, do you hear it?"

"Hear what, son?"

"I hear a car!"

We strained to hear something besides the wind whipping the bare tree branches, and sure enough, we all heard the unmistakable hum of an engine. We only heard it for a few seconds, but that was enough. Jim led us toward where the sound had come from. Within half an hour the woods thinned out, and we soon stepped onto the snow-covered road.

We made it out with only numb fingers, toes, and noses. To our amazement, we looked down the road and saw that we had emerged from the woods about fifty yards from our truck. What a wonderful sight!

After offering a prayer of thanksgiving for deliverance from what could have been a deadly situation, we headed to the truck and home. We were thankful for the faith of a child—faith not only in his earthly father but also in his heavenly Father. We also knew we would be more prepared the next time we ventured into the woods.

Some might say it was sure lucky we heard that vehicle. I don't think it was luck at all. We'd heard no sound from cars or trucks traveling that road before our time of prayer. I believe God answered our prayer by sending a vehicle down that snow-covered road just when we needed to hear a sound to lead us home. When God's children cry out to Him for help, He is quick to respond. We were all reminded that there is power in prayer.

And who knows? Maybe one of our guardian angels was driving that car.

An Earthquake Full of Blessings

AnnaLee Conti

The car door slammed behind me as Carol, Linda, and I dashed up the steps. As we entered the kitchen, Carol's mother asked, "Have you girls been watching TV?"

"No," Carol said. "Why?"

"I know AnnaLee grew up in Alaska." Her mother nodded toward me and gestured toward the television. "A few minutes ago, a news bulletin said the main street of Anchorage has been leveled by an earthquake."

"Oh, it must be an exaggeration." I laughed. "We have earthquakes all the time."

Just then, the announcer again interrupted the programming: "And now for the latest on the earthquake that hit south central Alaska early this evening." We listened to a report by telephone from Fort Greeley.

167

I was eighteen years old, and was visiting the home of a classmate during Easter vacation of my freshman year at Seattle Pacific College. Although I had grown up in a missionary family in Alaska and loved my home state, I was following my dream of attending a Christian college where I could enjoy fellowship with young people my own age and find a husband who shared my faith. To me, that had meant leaving Alaska.

Now, without warning, in a matter of minutes, my home was a disaster area.

I listened for news of Seward, where my family lived.

"The port city of Seward, 120 miles south of Anchorage by car, has been wiped off the map by tsunamis, and the town is entirely engulfed by fire," the report continued.

As the full impact of those awful words hit me, I groaned. Did I still have a family? Had our home been destroyed? What would I do if my folks had been killed?

These questions and more played through my mind like a tape recording, but I was powerless to do anything but pray, "Oh, God, help them!"

I spent a sleepless night in front of the television and endless days listening anxiously to every news report and reading every newspaper. With each attempt to call home, I received the same robotic reply: "I'm sorry. Your call cannot be completed due to the Alaska earthquake."

When would I hear from my family?

Back at school, I checked the mail the instant it was distributed. At church, I heard that a minister friend of our family had died when the dock where he worked as a longshoreman in Valdez had collapsed. Since my father supplemented his meager church income by working as a longshoreman, my fear increased to near panic.

The Good Friday Earthquake, centered in Prince William Sound, had registered 9.2 on the Richter scale—the strongest recorded earthquake to ever hit North America. It had wreaked havoc on every city, town, and village in south central Alaska and had shredded connecting roads.

Finally, a letter arrived. With trembling fingers, I tore open the envelope addressed in my father's handwriting and read quickly. Everyone was safe.

"Thank you, God!" I breathed.

Weak with relief, I sank into a chair to read my mother's postscript, which described their harrowing experiences.

To keep from being thrown to the floor when the violent shaking began, they had grabbed doorposts or anything else solid. The hard jolts seemed to go on and on. The earthquake lasted only five minutes, but that was a long time when they thought the house might collapse or that the undulating ground might crack open and swallow them.

When the quaking subsided, they ran outside. Smoke billowed hundreds of feet into the air from the huge oil storage tanks a few blocks away. The ruptured tanks belched burning oil that was being channeled through town along the railroad tracks. The quake generated an immediate tsunami that spread the raging inferno throughout the entire industrial area along the waterfront.

To flee the flames, the 1,800 residents of Seward jumped into their cars and drove toward the lagoon, where cliffs on one side and the bay on the other straddled a two-lane road, the only route out of town. Traffic slowed to a crawl. Bumper to bumper, they inched along.

Midway across, my mother noticed that railroad cars and boats were being pushed up and over the breakwater as though by a giant hand. Puzzled, then horrified as everything raced toward them, she screamed, "Tsunami! Drive faster!"

My dad swerved into the empty inbound lane and passed the creeping line of cars. Waves swirled around the tires. Their car was the last to make it across before the tsunami crashed across the road, sweeping away cars and smashing houses, boats, and railroad cars against the cliffs like toys in a bathtub, and snapping sturdy trees like toothpicks.

Still the nightmare continued. Burning debris from the exploding oil tanks rode the crest of the second tsunami, setting the forest at the head of the bay on fire. It spread quickly. About three miles out of town, the traffic stopped abruptly. Word passed from car to car: "The bridges are out!" They had been thrust eight to twelve feet above the broken roadway. The people were trapped.

Just when it seemed they would all be incinerated, a third tsunami swept in and extinguished the fire. They spent the long, cold, sleepless night in the home of friends in a development near the bridges.

When they returned home the next day, they found the church and attached parsonage still standing. They were fortunate. Everything south of their block was gone. The oil tanks burned for days. Homes would be without electricity, water, sewer, and heat for weeks until the ground thawed enough to allow repairs.

The Seward I returned home to that summer was nothing like the thriving port town I had left the previous fall. More than eighty homes had been destroyed and thirty lives lost. The docks, railroad yards, boat harbor, warehouses, and canneries had been swept into Resurrection Bay, stripping the waterfront of all industry.

Then I realized how much the Great Alaska Earthquake had affected my life. I had worked several shifts in the shrimp cannery during high school and had planned to work there that summer to pay for my second year at Seattle Pacific College. But the cannery had vanished into the bay. With the docks gone, so was my father's supplemental income. My two younger siblings still lived at home and didn't have the financial resources to help. Family men couldn't find employment, let alone a single girl with little training. With mothers unemployed, too, I couldn't even get a baby-sitting job. My one-year scholarship and savings had been used, and I had already taken a loan out for my first year.

Would I even be able to continue my college education? Nothing short of a miracle would enable me to go to *any* college in the fall. As the jobless summer progressed, I tried to believe God for a miracle, but my hopes dwindled.

My heavenly Father had met my needs before. Just a few years earlier, I had won an all-expenses-paid trip to the United Nations, including a month-long, cross-country bus tour to New York City and back with thirty-five other teens. Summers in Alaska were cool, so I had no lightweight clothes for hot weather. My missionary family had no discretionary money, but we knew how to pray, and God had supplied the funds for every article of clothing I needed.

And there was the time four years earlier when our family had first moved to Seward—the airplane tickets and moving expenses had taken all of our money so we couldn't even stock the pantry. One day, my mother had no food to serve us for lunch. All morning she prayed.

Just before noon, a woman from the church called and asked my parents to baby-sit her children after school since she had to make an unexpected trip to Anchorage. A few minutes later, she arrived with the children—and a large bag of groceries and some cash. In the bag, my mother found all the ingredients except bread for bacon-lettuce-tomato sandwiches, a favorite meal we could rarely afford. My father hurried to the store. Just in time, God had supplied not only our lunch but a treat, too.

Another time, my parents planned to take the church youth to a rally. We had already gathered at the parsonage, when my dad told us there was no money for gas. We all held hands and prayed. The doorbell rang, and a man rushed in. "I don't know what's going on, but God prompted me to take my break now and come here to pay my tithe early."

I'd often experienced God's provision, but those needs seemed small compared to money for three years of college. I prayed and tried to have faith, but by late July, I was in despair. Then our church held a series of special services. I shared my concern with the visiting evangelists.

"Nothing's too big for God," they said, and my faith grew.

The first week of August, our neighbor, the local librarian, asked me to help her catalog a shipment of new books for the library. "Two hours a day for two weeks, but I can only pay you fifty cents an hour," she said apologetically.

Fall was approaching rapidly. Time was running out. The job wouldn't pay my way to college, but I was happy to have something useful to do.

During the second week I worked at the library, a bulletin arrived from the Ford Foundation. The librarian showed it to me. "I think you'll be interested in this."

It announced that a scholarship had been set up for those who had lost family members, property, or employment due to the Good Friday Earthquake. The scholarship would cover up to full expenses according to the student's need.

I was eligible.

There was only one catch. This scholarship was available only to those attending the two universities in Alaska.

Although I was disappointed that I could not go back to Seattle Pacific College, I knew this was God's answer to my prayers. I decided to apply to the University of Alaska in Fairbanks, and immediately felt peace that I had chosen the right path. At least I would be able to continue my education.

Days before school started in September, I received my letter of acceptance, a scholarship covering full expenses for the year, and notification that all of my credits had transferred.

And that's not all. Seward, located in the coastal region of south central Alaska, has much milder winters than Fairbanks, where winter temperatures often dip to 50 and 60 degrees below zero for extended periods of time. I needed a fur parka but didn't have one. A well-made, moderately priced parka cost about $500, and I had no money. The scholarship covered the purchase of the parka, as well as all of my books, and even some spending money. Three years later, I graduated from the University of Alaska debt free.

Not only did God provide me with a college education, He also gave me the desire of my heart. The first week at the University of Alaska that fall of 1964, I attended an InterVarsity Christian Fellowship meeting on campus and met a tall, handsome young man named Bob Conti. Three weeks after we graduated in 1967, we married and have served the Lord together ever since.

I often laughingly say, "God had to send an earthquake to answer my prayers to meet the man who would become my husband."

The Message From Heaven

BETTY JOHNSON DALRYMPLE

T he funeral was over. The house was empty. I was alone—more alone than I'd ever been. Richard had always been there for me. We had been high school sweethearts, raised three children, and spent our time together whenever possible. He was my safe haven.

And God had always been there for me, too. He had been my companion during my early years and His presence had seen me through those difficult teenage months—during my father's death and my mother's depression.

God's presence also gave me courage when I responded to the surgeon's shocking announcement, "There is no hope. Your husband's cancer has metastasized. He has days, maybe weeks, hopefully a few months."

"What?" I stammered. "We are a family of faith. There is always hope."

This man in the green surgeon's scrubs does not understand, I thought. *Our prayers will be answered. We'll experience a miracle, and the cancer will go into remission. Maybe Richard won't live to be ninety as we'd planned. But he is not going to die. Not my big, healthy, I-can-do-anything husband.*

During the following weeks, I prayed. Our family prayed. Our fellow church members prayed. Our friends all over the country prayed. How could we not experience a miracle with all of these people praying?

There was no miracle and no remission. On a cold January morning, four months after the surgeon's shocking news, we were back in the hospital, and I was sleeping on a cot in the corner of Richard's room. I was awakened and led from the room while the doctor whispered, "Mrs. Johnson, your husband isn't breathing—his heart has stopped."

Stunned, I just sat on the stool and cried. *Where is my miracle, God? How did this happen? I was sleeping right here, and I didn't hear him. Did he call for me? I never told him good-bye. God, didn't you hear my prayers?*

Those questions haunted me during the first days, but I was too busy with friends and family staying with me, so I didn't spend any quiet time listening for God's answers.

Then came the night when I was finally totally alone. Tears poured from my eyes as I began to shout, *"Where are you, God? Do you hear me? Please, please help me. I'm begging you. If you've ever loved me, if you love me now, somehow, some way, show me."*

Desperately I grabbed the booklet on my nightstand that my friend had brought to me the day Richard died.

"I was at Lisa's house when I received the call about Richard's passing," Bonnie had explained. "Lisa's husband died last year, and she said this booklet brought her great comfort. She sent it for you to read."

I'd read pages from it the previous night and found a bit of comfort in its message. It prodded me to trust in God.

Tonight I wanted more than comfort. I wanted answers. "Do you have a message in here for me tonight, God?" I sputtered between sobs. When I opened the booklet, a small card fluttered to the floor.

"Where did this come from?" I mumbled. "I didn't see this in the book last night or the other day when Bonnie gave it to me."

I picked up the card, noticed the picture of Jesus on the one side, turned it over, and read the words written on the back. It began by telling me that Richard was safely home in heaven.

"It's a message from Richard," I whispered. I continued reading, "He's telling me that all the pain and grief is over and he's at peace. God heard me. He heard my prayers."

Then, the answers I'd so desperately sought began rolling out of the words as I read on. They reassured me that Richard was not alone as he passed through the valley of the shadow of death. Jesus' love brightened his pathway.

"Oh, thank you, God. Thank you! Richard wasn't alone. I believe Jesus was with him," I cried. Now my tears had turned to tears of joy. I wanted to call someone, to share this wonderful news, but it was midnight.

A voice inside me broke into my time of joy. *I think you need to savor this moment, hold these reassurances close to your heart. You need to deepen your faith in your Father's will.*

A feeling of peace I have rarely experienced settled in my mind and soul. Finally, I read on and was told that my work is still unfinished, and when it is completed and God calls me home, Richard will receive me with joy.

Wow! When God answered my prayers that night, it was an awesome experience. I did not know then, and I do not know now, where that little three-by-five card was hiding during the previous night's reading. How did I not see it? And how did Bonnie just happen to be at her friend's house on the day of Richard's death? God knew what I needed, and He knew when I'd need it most.

God heard my prayers and gave me answers. It wasn't the miracle I expected—the miracle of healing for Richard—but it was a healing miracle for me. It was a message for that night and for all of the days and years ahead.

The next time I cry out, and I'm sure there'll be a next time, "God, do you hear me?" I know He will be listening and I know He will answer.

The Nativity Baby

DAVID MICHAEL SMITH

*L*et the little children come to me, and do not hinder them, for the kingdom of God belongs to such as these" (Luke 18:16).

Right after Thanksgiving it begins. Families and couples, people of all ages and backgrounds, begin their annual pilgrimage to the local Christmas tree farm to tag the perfect tree for the festive yuletide season. And at Turning Pointe Farm near Hartly, Delaware, tagging trees is commonplace.

But miracles?

Well, that's what makes the holiday season so magical.

Born and raised in New York City, and later residents of northern New Jersey, Tom and Roseann Conlon were familiar with traffic gridlock, high crime rates, high taxes, and a lifestyle that was far from tranquil. But in 1986, they purchased thirty-six acres of wooded farmland in the fertile epicenter of Delaware and became part-time weekend farmers.

After building a cozy log cabin on their own slice of earthly heaven, they planted three thousand evergreen seedlings by hand and named their picturesque property Turning Pointe Farm. For nearly two decades they farmed the rich flat acreage and planted additional firs, pines, and spruces, until the fields were filled with beautiful boughs of greenery and trees that had matured to marketable heights.

After retiring in 2003, the Conlons moved to their Delaware farm and realized their long-time dream of operating their Christmas tree farm full time. Because they now had more time to work the land, trim and sell trees, and assemble beautiful wreaths and holiday centerpieces, Turning Pointe Farm became a place that brought broad smiles to those who patronized it every chilly December.

But when they put up the annual crèche in 2004, things got *really* interesting. The Conlons and their son-in-law built a platform and a three-sided rustic shelter, covered with greenery grown on the farm, for the nearly life-size figures. Each piece was made of resin that resembled natural stone. There was a welcoming, watchful angel; the precious sleeping infant Jesus; and His earthly parents, a noble Joseph and a kneeling, prayerful Mary. A young shepherd came with his sheep to adore the holy child, while the three Magi patiently awaited their turn to present their gifts. The holy scenery was breathtaking.

Roseann was the inspiration behind the manger. She wanted to bring the reason for the season to tangible, meaningful life for her six grandchildren and to keep the holiday's focus on the virgin birth of the Son of God. So the day after Thanksgiving, the Conlon grandchildren carefully carried the still participants to the manger and set up the nativity. Then they added a large stone to the display with the word *Blessings* carved in it.

After the nativity scene was erected, Roseann and her husband told tree shoppers about it. People who wanted to could go to the manger and silently offer any prayer requests they had. And many did. At the same time, her grandchildren, ranging in age from three to eleven, prayed daily for all the people and their petitions. For the young prayer warriors, it was a faith-maturing ministry of goodwill.

The Conlon grandchildren didn't often know the exact requests, but occasionally someone would mention his or her need to Roseann. They prayed for people struggling with cancer, sickness, and disease. They prayed for broken relationships. They prayed for people suffering with depression, a common ailment during the holiday season.

But one desperate plea at the crèche stood out that first year.

Eric and Stephanie lived nearby and had frequented the farm. They were a fairly young couple, married for ten years and in their mid-thirties, with no children.

But they wanted children. Their hearts ached for children. For ten years they'd tried every off-the-wall piece of advice from friends, neighbors, and family. They tried ovulation kits. They tried fertility drugs. They tried medical procedures like IVF and artificial insemination in an effort to have a baby and start a family.

And they prayed for a miracle, *their* miracle—one about seven or eight pounds, twenty inches long, and a grin to die for.

But absolutely nothing worked.

To deepen their sorrow, Stephanie's mother had cancer and a prognosis shrouded in darkness. Stephanie had always hoped her mother would live long enough to tenderly hold her grandchild and smile into the eyes of the little bundle that would carry on the family heritage, but it appeared this hope was wishful fantasy.

After the couple picked out a Christmas tree, a statuesque Douglas fir, they quietly walked to the manger. Roseann watched from afar and diverted foot traffic while the hurting woman and her husband clasped hands and bowed their heads. The Christ child in the crib seemed to reach toward the husband and wife, as if to welcome their petitions. They were only there for a few minutes, and then they left. No one knew of their prayer appeal except God.

Christmas came and went, and another year had passed. Soon it was cold again and Christmas was gently energizing the winter.

Roseann was in her gift shop working on holiday wreaths when the door opened. It was Eric and Stephanie—another year older, but with one noticeable difference. They appeared radiant and taller, as if they had grown like the hundreds of evergreens at Turning Pointe Farm. They bustled into the shop to blurt out their story, a miracle, but as Stephanie's heavy woolen coat parted, Roseann knew the story. Stephanie was quite pregnant!

"We prayed for a baby at your nativity last year!" Stephanie exclaimed with tears in her eyes. "We were distraught and sad, but standing there looking down at Jesus, we felt hope."

Roseann hugged the happy couple and then explained the motivation behind assembling the crèche, which was back up for the new Christmas season. And she told the soon-to-be parents about her grandchildren's faithful prayers, intercessory pleas made to the Creator on the behalf of total strangers.

"And guess when I'm due!" Stephanie added with a grin. Eric interjected, "Christmas! December twenty-fifth!"

When the faith of little children, or those who come as children, is on display, God cannot remain idle. Miracles, healings, blessings, and acts of wonder become the norm. Just ask Eric and Stephanie, and they'll gladly tell you all about their handsome little boy, the best Christmas gift they will ever know.

The Miraculous Ride

JENNI DAVENPORT

H ey, I enjoyed seeing Hunter at camp this summer," Cal
exclaimed when I ran into him at the restaurant. Cal
runs a Christian youth camp where we've sent our
kids every year. A frown lined Cal's forehead as he continued.
"You know, he seemed a lot different this summer . . ."

Cal didn't have to go into more detail. I knew exactly what
he meant. Over the past few years, I'd seen my son go from a
boy who loved Jesus and asked Him into his heart at an early
age, to a good moral teen who was totally disconnected from
church and Christianity. In fact, it had been hard for me to get
my almost-eighteen-year-old to go to camp that summer before
his senior year.

"Please pray for him, Cal," I said. And I meant it. My heart
had long been burdened for my son's spiritual walk. I had quietly asked family and close friends to pray for Hunter. I work
at a Christian organization, and every week as part of our staff

meeting, we each place a prayer request in the middle of the table. At the end of the meeting, we each take a request and pray for it during the week.

Each week I'd put Hunter's name down as my prayer request. I might add other things, but I always asked my co-workers to pray for my son to walk in faith with God.

It wasn't that Hunter was a prodigal. He was a good, intelligent, moral kid who respected us and respected boundaries. His worst vice was the bad language that would sometimes float from his upstairs room where he was frequently gaming or hanging out with his friends.

Besides asking others to pray for Hunter, of course, I often prayed for my son during my long commutes to work and at other times when his soul was foremost in my mind.

I also talked to him. Hunter was always polite, but I would often see him zone out when I spoke about faith matters. Sometimes, I saw his mouth tighten in disagreement. But I kept looking for opportunities to engage with my son spiritually. Sometimes, I subtly brought up topics, and other times I was blunt so he'd know where I stood and how I felt. I asked the Lord to help me speak outside of the clichés to better help my postmodern son connect. It was one of those times that he let it all out. We were talking about his not wanting to go to church and avoiding anything with a spiritual focus when the flow started.

"I just don't know if I believe in God anymore," he announced, practically trembling with emotion. "It all just seems so unbelievable."

More than his words at the moment, I was struck by his countenance. He seemed so terrified to talk about it. *"He's afraid you're going to yell at him, that you're not going to love him as much if he can't believe,"* a voice seemed to tell me.

So I just listened with an open heart, and he gained confidence to tell me more. He went on with a few specifics, parroting some of the things I imagine he'd heard at school and from his older friends.

Finally, I spoke. "Hunter, it's okay to have a hard time believing. God can handle your questions. God can handle your doubts. God is big enough. It's okay to question Him. That's how we get to know Him."

While I spoke confidently, my heart wept. And I redoubled my prayer efforts on Hunter's behalf. My burden grew, and in the coming days I told the Lord, "I just can't handle it if Hunter doesn't know you. Oh, Lord, please draw my son to you."

It probably sounds crazy, but I was also burdened when I thought of the end times. I'm not a big end-of-the-world panicker. At my age, I've lived through times when Christians have gotten worked up and made predictions about the rapture and end times. I'm not real dogmatic on when or how the church will be raptured or when and how Jesus is going to return. But I do believe the signs might be ripe in our world for the end times foretold in the Bible (I figure either the new earth or a revival is ahead). I was raised in the middle of the rapture focus in the '70s, so I lean toward that theology.

"Oh, Lord, what if the rapture happens before Hunter is ready to meet you face-to-face? He's driving now; what if he gets in a car wreck and dies?"

I didn't always focus on such things, but they did come to my mind at times, and I continued to pray . . . and to worry. The older two stepchildren my husband, Rick, and I had raised had fallen from their faith in their late teens (which made me fret about our parenting skills—or lack thereof!). They had walked more on the wild side than my son, but we had been blessed to see them come back to Christ with a passion—one was studying to be a missionary and one was winning her in-laws to Christ right and left.

It's not like I haven't been through this before, I thought. But somehow it was different. We'd instilled more Scripture in the older ones. We'd been younger and more active in ministry. Some of that passion had decreased because of job situations and my husband's chronic health issues.

The world had changed a lot since the older two were teen-agers. The battle against Christianity seemed so much stronger. And the older two weren't intellectuals—they didn't face the questions that Hunter was facing. Theirs was more of a tem-porary rebellion than an intellectual rejection of the gospel. I'd prayed and cared for them—probably even more than they realize today—but they didn't quite cause the angst in me that Hunter's spiritual coldness did. Hunter is our only boy, and everyone knows how mothers and sons are tied together. Could I really leave Hunter in the Holy Spirit's hands?

The days passed after Hunter's outburst, and outwardly I went on as normal—loving him, praying for him, and looking for opportunities to point him to God. Was the Holy Spirit getting through at all? I couldn't tell.

And then God answered my prayer in a way I never could have imagined! I was raised with Nazarene and Baptist influ-ences. Whether good or bad, people in my faith culture don't often experience dramatic or unusual signs and wonders—I often envy my charismatic friends! So the last thing I expected God to do was to give me a dream.

I hadn't gone to bed that night with my mind on Hunter's spiritual state, so the dream wasn't arising from anything in my immediate subconscious mind. I hadn't eaten spicy food, hadn't done anything particularly spiritual before I went to bed. Just took my melatonin and was out quickly.

It was toward morning when the dream started. My husband was driving our family somewhere, as he often did. I was in the passenger's seat and our two youngest kids were in the back seat.

Suddenly, something seemed to be happening. The top of the car disappeared, and it became the convertible my husband and I had always wanted. As Rick continued to drive, the car lifted off the ground. A light filled my heart and filled the sky as I realized Jesus had come for us and was drawing us to Him. We got to take the scenic route. The car flew over valleys and streams and mountains and oceans.

But there was something beyond the beauty and light—there was an indescribable joy. I've had a lot of happy times in my life, but this was something I've never experienced. It was like all of creation was bursting with joy and light and life.

And the best part was that my children were in the back seat. They were with us. We were being raptured and our children were there.

The car continued to be drawn by an invisible force, like a Star Wars tractor beam. We were eventually pulled through clouds and into a world that was rising as we watched. As houses appeared, the car pulled into a driveway of a modest, pretty little home—not the mansion by the mountains and ocean that I've hoped for, but I didn't care. My family was together and we were in whatever world Jesus inhabited.

The dream ended. It was so wonderful, so peaceful, that I tried to stay in a dozy state and call it back. But no luck. It had served its purpose. I woke up.

As I lay there, it was almost like my soul was coming out of anesthesia. My body was awake, but it was as if my spirit was still lingering in the land of confident peace, the land it was made for.

As I floated back to earth mentally, I surprised myself by bursting into tears. I'm not an overly emotional person—I tend to be too pragmatic for my own good. I only cry when I'm very upset about something. But this time it wasn't tears of distress or disappointment. For the first time in my life, I was crying for joy.

I didn't tell my husband or anyone about the dream. One reason was that I'm a Nazarene/Baptist girl with a skeptical heart—only one other time in my life had God clearly spoken to me in a dream. The other reason was that whenever I even thought about the dream, I'd start crying—I couldn't have explained why, and still can't explain why tears flow whenever I think about it.

I didn't have to ponder to know that the dream was given to me by God, or what it meant. The dream meant God had heard my pleas and my tears for my son, that He understood my burden for Hunter. He was showing me that it's going to be okay. That He has His hand on Hunter and is drawing him to himself. He showed me Hunter is indeed His child.

So I still talk to Hunter about his spiritual journey. But now I can do so in confidence, knowing God is working. I still pray for Hunter fervently, that God will become real to him and make him a godly man. I still pray that God will guard his steps and protect him from the wrong influences.

But now I don't pray with fear and panic. I pray with hope and reassurance, with the faith and confidence that my hopes will be realized. For a short time, I experienced the joy and light of heaven, and I know Hunter will experience it, too.

Nowhere to Call Home

BOBBIE ROPER

For most people, retirement is a bit scary, but senior folks usually have a house, with or without a mortgage. We live in the sunny state of Florida, where many residents have not one house, but two. They have one up north for the warmer months, and one here when the snow chases them south.

We were not so fortunate. My husband, Jim, was a pastor for over thirty years. His churches were small congregations in rural areas of New York, Pennsylvania, North Carolina, and Florida. Though the salary was low by most standards, all the churches provided a parsonage, so we always had a place to live.

When Jim reached age sixty-six, and started drawing Social Security, we realized that retirement was right around the corner, as well as the possibility of major health issues that could keep him from performing his duties as a pastor. If he suddenly needed to leave the ministry, what would we do? An even more serious thought was what would I do if he had a major heart attack that took his life?

We had sold our home in South Carolina thirty-one years earlier, enabling us to attend Bible college, so we had nowhere to call home. Our denomination has several retirement communities for pastors, there are government-subsidized facilities for low-income people, and of course there are our children. Feasible options for some, perhaps, but not for us.

Our prayer was pretty simple: "Lord, retirement is close and we have nowhere to call home. Please show us your plan."

God had provided for our family in so many miraculous ways over the years, but what would He do now? James 1:5 says, "If any of you lacks wisdom, you should ask God, who gives generously to all without finding fault, and it will be given to you."

So we asked for wisdom.

First, we had to decide where we wanted to live. We have four grown children. Two live in Florida, fairly close to where we were living, and two live up north. North was not an option, because Jim is a southern boy and had a difficult time dealing with the snow and cold. Being an avid saltwater fisherman, he wanted to be close to the water so he could spend his retirement years fishing. We finally decided on the west coast of Florida, a little farther north of us in an area called the Nature Coast.

Jim began to search the Internet for homes in that area. As he searched for a place that wasn't too far from the water, I prayed for a place in the woods. His soul is refreshed breathing in the salt air, while mine is renewed listening to the wind whistling through the trees and soaking in the wonderful sights, sounds, and smells of God's fabulous creation.

Psalm 37:4 says, "Take delight in the Lord, and he will give you the desires of your heart." I was wondering how God was going to do that when we had different desires.

Over the next months, Jim lined up places to look at. We knew our retirement income wouldn't amount to much, so we needed a place with a low mortgage payment. We needed a place with a shed. Jim dabbles in woodworking, so he wanted enough land to have a workshop. We also needed space for two vehicles and his flatboat. A porch would be nice, since we have his grandfather's wooden swing—an heirloom close to a hundred years old.

We looked at houses on our days off, but most of what we found didn't have useable acreage or the price wasn't workable.

Sometime in October, Jim lined up three properties. The first one was on two acres. It was a beautiful property, but the house was small with no storage building or garage. Since we were in the same area as the third property, we decided to go by and look at it before our appointment with the realtor at the second property. We drove down an asphalt road that turned into dirt right at the edge of the property. It was a manufactured home (not what we wanted, but probably all we could afford) on two and a half acres.

We parked the car and sat there for a moment taking it all in. There was a large storage building. Across half of the house front was a large screened porch that wrapped around to a side door. Scrub oaks intermingled with pine trees filled most of the front and side yards, as well as the area behind the house.

As Jim walked the back area, I felt at home. When Jim came back to the car, he echoed the same words. Our dilemma was that the realtors had told us the property was under contract. A young couple was trying to buy it, but there had been many delays and problems with financing.

We drove to the second house on our list and arrived before the real estate agent got there. The house looked small and with the sloping back yard there was no place to put the workshop Jim needed. We called the realtor and told her we weren't interested.

Driving back to the "house in the woods," we wondered if this was the place for us. It seemed to fit what we both wanted. It was only about twenty minutes from the water, Jim's desire, and was sitting in the woods, fulfilling mine. If only someone else didn't already have dibs on it!

We drove to the back of the property, where the realtors met us. Jim told them we had looked around earlier and really liked what we saw on the outside. We would certainly be interested should the present contract fall through.

The Bible tells us in Philippians 4:19, "My God will meet all your needs according to the riches of his glory in Christ Jesus."

God knew that we needed a house to call home even before we prayed, so we shouldn't have been surprised when the realtors told us that the contract had expired at noon—it was now 1 p.m. We wanted to shout our praise to the Lord! Did He hold the house under contract until we could find it?

Some would say, "Really? You really believe that?"

Yes, I really believe that.

This is not the end of the story. Though the house needed much work inside, we knew this was a gift from God and an answer to prayer. We put in an offer, the sellers countered, and we accepted.

Now we had to get financing. We sat for hours at our bank trying to get a mortgage. Their computers were down, then slow—on and on it went until we finally had the loan papers in hand. After looking them over, we didn't see how we could possibly make the payments, and when we looked at the interest and what we would actually be paying for the house, we were flabbergasted.

We looked at each other, feeling deflated, not knowing what to do. We didn't believe God would have us get into debt like that, and we would probably both have to hold down full time jobs till the mortgage was paid in thirty years. We would be in our nineties! We left the bank after telling the loan officer that we needed to think about it.

As we talked and prayed about it, God supplied the answer. Each denominational church Jim had served had put a small monthly amount into a retirement fund for him. Over twenty-plus years that amount had grown, and without our even realizing it, God had been providing the money we needed to pay cash for our retirement home. We bought when the market was low and the property needed a lot of work, so the price was almost ridiculous for two and a half acres. But most important, God's hand was in it.

And that's not the end of the story, either. The Lord allowed us to work for the next nine months, which gave us the opportunity to put our Social Security into a building fund so we could make repairs. We closed on the house in November, and traveled the two hours back and forth on our days off and vacation to work on it.

We retired in June, and moved to our house in the woods on July 4. There was enough money left in the retirement fund for Jim to purchase the workshop he wanted with a few dollars left.

Every once in a while, Jim checks the Internet to see if there's anything comparable to our house-in-the-woods gift from God. Nothing even comes close. How awesome is our God!

Leaving the God of Money

MARLEEN MCDOWELL

"Where, Lord? Where is that victorious life you promised?" I pleaded for an answer as I drove to work. Tears poured down my face, blurring my vision of the road. This had gone on so long the pain was too much to bear.

For years, our finances had been an endless roller coaster ride. We both worked and made enough for a comfortable living, but instead we were always broke, always struggling, always worrying, and always fighting. Uphill, downhill. In debt, out of debt. *We had just finished the long, slow, laborious climb out of debt, and here we were again, speeding over the suicide drop to the pit of easy credit.*

So many times I had prayed for the Lord to change my husband, but now, ten years into the marriage, nothing was different. Repeatedly, promises were made and broken. Talking, pleading, reasoning gave way to blaming, shaming, and threats.

The situation was hopeless. Why didn't God answer me? What was wrong? Did I need to pray more? Should I fast?

But we know God hears us. And God did hear it—all of it. He was just waiting for me to hear Him! That day as I cried my way to work, God answered my prayer. A voice spoke in my mind: *"If your happiness depends on the balance in your checkbook, you will continue to be miserable."*

I was shocked. This wasn't fair! I wasn't the one who spent all the money. My mouth opened. I tried to explain, but I could only repeat what I had just heard: *"If your happiness depends on the balance in your checkbook, you will continue to be miserable."*

Yes, I admitted, my moods did rise and fall with my bank balance. After all, it was stressful when the money wasn't there and the bills were coming in. My husband and I were so different! I wasn't the problem! I was a responsible person! I was a good steward! I wanted to save our money. Wasn't that what we were supposed to do? Certainly, my way was better! Everything would be fine if my husband would only listen to me!

As I defended myself, I fought against the truth that was forming in my mind.

Something was wrong. Money was *too* important to me. It was my security. It was the answer to my problems. It meant more to me than my husband or my marriage or . . . The thought forced its way into my mind and I could not deny it: I trusted money more than I trusted the Lord. There it was. The ugly truth—money was my god.

Here I was, feeling self-righteous and putting all the blame on my husband. Yet I was the one with a serious problem. I was breaking the first commandment: "You shall have no other gods before me." Yet here I was, worshiping a money-idol. My sin was directly against God!

With the truth in the open, a choice lay before me. I could continue to cling to my money-idol and ultimately destroy our marriage, or I could turn to the Lord and trust Him to deliver me from my troubles.

I made my decision and the helplessness dissolved. The tears started again, only this time they were tears of repentance.

That evening, I admitted my sin to my husband. I asked for his prayers and his help to tear down my idol with a money fast. For one month, I would not touch money in any form. He agreed to pick up my paycheck, take care of the bills, do the grocery shopping, put gas in my car, and handle all financial matters.

It was a long month. Co-workers invited me to lunch, friends asked me to go shopping, but each time a polite "Not today" excused me from the activity.

Frustration filled the first week as I automatically reached for my purse before I remembered it was empty. The second week, I was a bit resentful as I marked time waiting for the month to end. Yet by the third week, acceptance began to set in and it wasn't such a big deal anymore.

A slow change was happening. I found that since I wasn't involved in the finances, the worries and responsibilities no longer consumed me. My mood stabilized. By the end of the month, the bondage to my idol was broken and joy was becoming my shy companion.

However, that was not the only blessing God had for me. For a time, the roller coaster continued to storm around the track. On the steep downhill rides, I learned to seek the Lord first and to stay in the Word as He taught me to put my trust in Him so I could have peace whether the bank account was flush or had a zero balance. While we were in the pit of easy credit, He taught me to be thankful for the small things and to be content with what I already possessed rather than dwell on what I could not buy.

I learned that God can work all things for our good, just as He used my husband's financial weakness to change me. That taught me to look deeper into our problems in order to search out the hidden blessings. Most important, He taught me to take the log out of my own eye before I looked for the splinter in my husband's eye.

God is faithful. As I repented of my sin, He began to heal my husband's past hurts and deal with the mismanagement of our finances. Today, after more than forty years of marriage, we are retired and our income is half of what it was—yet we feel rich. Our wealth is not in our bank account, but in the treasury of our strong marriage and our walk with the Lord.

So many times when the situation looked hopeless and the pain was too much, I wanted to take the easy way out and run away from that wild ride. Today, I am thankful that both of us chose to stay and work through the problems, because during that wild ride God gave us the tools to live a victorious life.

Paper Angels

BETH DUEWEL

I felt as if I'd met her before. Her gestures were calm and familiar. She was knitting when I burst into the room and interrupted her rhythm with a wail. Past the point of pain I could bear, I crossed the threshold into the small waiting room while suffering a moment of untamed grief.

Normally, I would have been self-conscious about such a dramatic show of tears. But on a normal day I wouldn't be saying good-bye to my momma. On a normal day I wouldn't have to leave the bedside of the one who had tucked me in, and know I would never see her again on this earth.

I was completely mad at myself. Frustrated that I was too weak to stay and hold her hand through those last moments, I ran to the family waiting room to cry alone. The room had been empty and had provided an echoing silence all weekend. It was a quiet respite with tiny chairs and outdated magazines.

But then I saw her.

She didn't seem upset that I was a maniac. She glanced over her glasses as if she had been expecting me.

At twenty years old, I couldn't help but feel a little robbed. My heart already missed my mom. My friends would have their mothers around to answer questions about how to make meatloaf and what to do with a colicky baby. As if those were major concerns. Either way, I wouldn't know how to do them— at least not the way my mom did.

I plopped down in a rust-colored chair, trying not to wail *too* loudly and disturb the tiny cubicle of peace. Jerry, my husband of a year, had stayed behind with my mom, dad, and uncle. He was the brave one. He was saying good-bye to a woman who'd become his second mother.

My mom had been unhappy until he called her by what she felt to be her deserved name. "Jerry, you need to call me Mom—I won't answer to anything else." She had been determined to nurture his heart.

Jerry had lost his mom at the age of eight; many memories of his mother had faded like a sun-bathed watercolor. And my mom, raising three girls with hormones and bad-hair days, was anxious to claim another son-in-law. Calm and collected, Jerry's moods were as level as well-placed bricks. Jerry and Mom were a great fit.

And now I didn't know how I would replace the piece missing in both of our lives.

I'm not quite sure when it happened—maybe when I closed my eyes—but the knitting-lady was no longer knitting. She was tending to me in the worn chair next to mine. Apparently she was ready to console my fears.

Her voice was seamless as her words sewed stitches into my heart. I saw her curly silver hair through the puddles in my eyes. Her hair was like my mom's, soft and uniform in color. She didn't appear worried that I might wrinkle her as she pulled me close. And with her sweet hushes, I was a little girl again.

As my mind traveled back, I could hear my mom call my name while she stood on our cement porch. My favorite snack, celery sticks slathered with peanut butter, waited for me inside.

Earlier that morning, I hadn't wanted to go to school. At the bus stop, I held on to the stop sign, my normally compliant body refusing to let go, while I pushed the patience of the bus driver, who beat on the horn. Kindergarten can be tough for an insecure four-year-old, I suppose. My anxious body melted into the steel pole while Mom in her red robe and fuzzy slippers came to my rescue.

It could have ended badly. But it didn't. I could have been scolded in front of the last two streets of kids, their noses stuck tight to the windows. But I wasn't. Instead, my mom's words were calm and secure, "Let's go home, Beth-Anne."

Her fingers gently peeled me from the pole while she stroked my tear-soaked hair.

The woman, hands void of knitting needles, pushed back the wet hair that stuck to my cheeks. "Oh, my dear child, your mom loves you very much." Her words floated like a hummed lullaby. "God loves you."

For the next however-many minutes, she reassured me of God's love and plan for my life. It was as if she knew me. Or that she knew I had read Psalm 23 to my mom earlier that day and was reciting it back to me in a palpable way.

My mom and I had been alone together in her room, a room awake with alarms and respirator puffs, while her body slept in a coma. The doctors assured me that she could hear. Our one-way conversation was intimate as words bounced off of the sterile sheets and sunk into my heart—words that peeled my anxious heart off of my stubborn will, promising calm pastures and a restored soul.

I wanted that. And in a hospital in the saddest of situations, I felt I could have it. I wish I'd have been more observant that day. But my senses were numb, as if dulled by the selfishness of grief. You would think that I'd have been very alert to a complete stranger. Especially one so willing to be used as a giant Kleenex. But there was no time for congenialities; my tears were interrupted by my husband's sobs trailing down the hall. He came in to tell me what I already knew: My mom was gone. A week before Christmas.

While I helped my father check out of a bed-and-breakfast that evening, the owner, hoping to console me for my loss, handed me a simple but appreciated gift—a paper angel.

That next day, I placed the gift on the top of our tree. It seemed the right spot for such a beautiful little item, as Christmas came quickly that year, leaving me with little motivation to decorate. After Christmas, Jerry, eager to lighten the load, offered to help wrap up the ornaments. That was usually not my favorite chore, and was even more daunting with my heavy heart.

Reaching to the top of the tree, I lifted the paper angel.

"Honey, do you remember the woman who was in the waiting room with me the day Mom died? I've been thinking about her."

Jerry stared at me as if straining to fill in the blanks. "What?"

Paper Angels

"You know—the woman sitting beside me when you came in—she had a bag with knitting needles and a blanket. I really don't know why I didn't introduce you, but I guess I didn't even ask her name . . ."

My voice trailed off as I remembered her words of comfort. My husband seemed confused, either with the wrapping of ornaments or the conversation. Or both.

"Honey, no one was with you in the waiting room; you were all by yourself when I came in."

And as I thought it through, I really didn't remember seeing her after he came in.

Hmmm. Now I was the confused one. *Had my mental state been so altered?*

No, I felt the touch of her hand—I heard her words. *But really, what color yarn was she knitting with? What was she wearing?*

Questions piled high in my mind. But thinking back, I was so wrapped up in the blanket of grief, I couldn't see through it. I guess everything seems a little blurry through a downpour of tears.

"No. She was there," I corrected. "She stroked my hair just like mom used to do. She talked to me about God's love and told me it would be okay. I'd have gone crazy without her."

My husband's sideways glance was all the confirmation I needed. He felt I already *had* gone crazy.

Logically, I recognized his dilemma. And I had to agree—it didn't make sense. But then again, life hadn't made much sense in a while. And true, there were no streams of light, nothing shiny or attention-grabbing about the woman who so willingly kept me company.

203

"Well, she was a godsend." My tone sounded cliché even to me.

I stared at the paper angel resting in my hand and traced its subtle etching and delicately placed halo. Suddenly it made perfect sense. I knew then that just one detail was missing from the paper angel—a tiny pair of knitting needles.

A Bright New World

JOYCE STARR MACIAS

I t was painful to see my father so weakened by disease. It didn't seem right that a man who had been so strong all his life now needed help to get out of his hospital bed.

But as much as I worried about the cancer spreading through his body, I was far more concerned about his spiritual state. I wanted to be sure he would be ready for heaven.

I knew both of my parents believed that God existed in a general sort of way, some kind of good God who lived too far away for ordinary people to reach. But I was sure they had no personal relationship with Jesus or even knew they could have one.

They were good parents—kind, moral people who taught my brother and me to be good citizens and to care about other people. Throughout my growing-up years, I remember times when they showed their respect for God in ways that sometimes seemed odd to me—like when my mother made us eat fish on Good Friday because it was something her Catholic friends did.

I was out of the house and married with three children before I heard the gospel for the first time and asked Jesus to forgive my sins and come into my life. The salvation I experienced that day changed me.

But I found it difficult to share my newfound faith with my mother and father. In the back of my mind, I'm sure I was thinking: *Who am I to be telling my parents what they need to do?*

But now that my father was so sick, I knew I had to share Jesus with him. At least I could try.

So before I left the hospital one evening, I got up my courage and asked, "Dad, may I pray for you before I leave?"

Instead of answering, he turned his head and stared at the wall of his hospital room.

I don't remember what I said after that, but I felt like a total failure. How could I share my faith with him before it was forever too late?

I lived about forty-five minutes away from my parents' home, and I tried to get there almost every night to see them. With a demanding full-time job, that wasn't always easy. I'd rush home, make supper for my family, and hit the road.

Since Dad was in and out of the hospital a lot, I often didn't know until the last minute whether I'd see him there or back at home. And I still had no idea how to approach him about spiritual matters.

I'd already tried one method that hadn't seemed to work. I had given him tape recordings of myself playing the piano and singing. Dad was always proud that I could play. We weren't wealthy, and I knew it must have been a sacrifice for my parents to pay for my piano lessons year after year.

I had recorded a mixture of traditional songs and classical pieces, like "Clair de Lune," that I knew he liked. In between, I would play and sing hymns that I hoped would touch his heart. My mother told me he liked to listen to them, but they didn't seem to be having the effect I'd prayed for.

One day, when I telephoned my mother after work, she seemed more upset than usual. Dad wasn't doing well, and she was worried. His long illness was clearly taking its toll on her.

"Dad's back in the hospital. I don't know what's going to happen," she said, her voice quivering. She asked if I could stay overnight with her.

I hadn't planned on going that night, but what could I say? I told her I'd get there in time to take her out to eat before we went to see Dad.

As I rushed to gather my things, I prayed that God would strengthen my mother and give her peace. And I prayed that my father would open his heart to the Lord.

Mom had pulled herself together by the time I arrived, but her swollen eyes showed me she'd been crying. Dad was alert enough to enjoy our time together, but I still felt tongue-tied when it came to talking to him about the Lord.

Back at the house, I headed for my old room, which was next to my parents' bedroom. I had barely settled down, when I heard Mom's voice: "Joyce, don't you usually read your Bible before you go to sleep?" she asked.

"Yes, I do, Mom."

"Would you mind coming in here and reading it to me?"

"Yes, of course," I answered, immediately changing my reading plan and choosing verses that would explain God's plan of salvation.

Mom listened intently as I read. She seemed so interested that I had no trouble asking if she had understood what the verses meant. When she said that she did, I asked her if she'd like to pray and give her life to Jesus.

With tears in her eyes, she nodded that she'd like to do that. For the first time, my mother and I prayed together. And when she lifted her head, I could see that something wonderful had happened. She had accepted Jesus as her Lord.

The whole world seemed brighter than ever as I drove to work early the next morning! My heart bubbled over with joy. I kept thanking God that Mom had given her heart to Jesus! I prayed that Dad would be next.

But weeks went by, and though Dad recovered enough to go back home for a while, the time never seemed right to talk to him about his spiritual condition.

One day, I drove to the town where my parents lived to attend a monthly meeting my denomination was holding. The meetings always began with a late afternoon service, followed by a meal provided by the host church, a fellowship time, and an evening service. This time, they substituted a prayer meeting for the second service. That was fine with me. If ever I needed to pray, it was now.

The host pastor led the prayer time, and I immediately felt God's presence more strongly than I ever had before. People began to pray out loud for their needs, something I usually felt uncomfortable about doing. But this time I joined in, asking God to open my father's heart to the gospel and to give me boldness.

I felt such freedom as I pleaded for my father's salvation, and I could hear others agreeing with me in prayer. I'd never felt such awareness of the Holy Spirit's presence! Suddenly, God showed me that my father would turn his life over to Jesus before he died. That message was as clear as if God had spoken the words out loud.

All at once, I knew what to do. I would go and see my father right away, even though I hadn't planned on going there that night.

Mom and I hugged before I went into the living room to see Dad. He was sitting in his swivel rocker next to a little end table. As always, he was reading a book.

I told him I believed God had sent me. My statement surprised him enough that he set his book aside. He remained silent as I told him how much God loved him and that He'd sent Jesus to pay the penalty for our sins, including his, on the cross.

His eyes stayed glued to me the whole time I spoke.

At last he's going to surrender his life to the Lord!

But he didn't. He wasn't angry or upset, but he didn't seem interested in what I'd said. I couldn't have been more disappointed.

I had envisioned him bowing his head and telling Jesus that he wanted to become his child. But he just thanked me for coming, hugged me, and went back to his book.

My heart ached as I drove home. But God let me know that I needed to leave the results to Him. I'd heard the expression "Let go and let God," but I had no idea that doing it could be so difficult.

"All right, Lord, I will believe you," I conceded as I turned into my driveway. "My father is in your hands. Only you can convince him of his need. I certainly can't."

The next day, I phoned a pastor I knew who lived closer to my parents' home, and he agreed to visit my father the next time Dad was hospitalized.

We didn't have to wait long. Mom called me a day or two later to say that my father had taken a turn for the worse. When I called the pastor, he assured me he'd visit my father every day and would pray for him.

I didn't get back to the hospital for a couple of days, due to icy road conditions, and by the time I next saw my father, he was so weak that he couldn't talk with me. But I could feel God's presence in the room, and I knew something supernatural was going on.

"Dad, is it all right if I pray with you?" I asked.

This time he didn't turn away. Tears streamed down both our faces as I prayed, asking God to give my father faith to believe in Jesus as his Lord and Savior.

Somehow, I knew that my prayer had been answered. My father couldn't utter the words to tell me, but I knew he had become a believer.

Here was the miracle I had sought for so long!

Within days, my father went home to be with the Lord. I was sure in my heart of the miracle that had taken place in his heart. But God in His mercy and kindness allowed me to hear more of the story.

During the funeral service, the pastor who had visited him spoke of my father's long involvement as a member of the Boy Scout council and his diligent work in developing a campground for the local Boy Scout troops.

I loved hearing the accolades about his scout work, but the words that followed soothed my heart.

"The motto of the Boy Scouts is to 'be prepared,'" the pastor said. "This man taught many young scouts that motto, but I want you to know that he had taken his own advice. He was prepared to meet God because of his personal faith in Jesus

Christ. He wasn't able to say the words out loud, but I can tell you that I'm certain he gave his heart to the Lord before he left this earth."

God gave me the miracle I had prayed so hard for. Some people call it a "death-bed conversion," but I know it was a miracle. A last-minute miracle that God accomplished by His supernatural power.

Miracle Boy

MELINDA WRIGHT, AS TOLD
TO ANITA ESTES

D o not be anxious about anything, but in every situation, by prayer and petition, with thanksgiving, present your requests to God. And the peace of God, which transcends all understanding, will guard your hearts and your minds in Christ Jesus."

The pastor had barely finished reading the verses, Philippians 4:6–7, when my phone rang. I answered, and heard the words in every parent's worst nightmare.

"Your son has been in a terrible accident. A car hit him head on and catapulted him off his bike into the air. He has multiple lacerations and fractures and is in severe condition. He's being airlifted to Rhode Island Hospital."

When I told my husband, Richie, he turned pale and felt numb, but my reaction was different.

What normally would strike fear in a parent's heart had the opposite effect on me. I felt a strong sense of God's presence. An incredible peace washed over me.

During the service, I'd been praying for another crisis, regarding my nephew, and afterward we received a text message that he was safe. I felt elated that God had answered our prayers so quickly. When the bad news came about our son, I felt God would do the same for him. I believed it was the perfect opportunity for us to put into practice Philippians 4:9 (another verse we had just heard): "Whatever you have learned or received or heard from me, or seen in me—put it into practice. And the God of peace will be with you."

As we drove the three and a half hours to Rhode Island, anxious thoughts tried to assault us. My son's landlord filled in the details, telling my husband that David had severe head trauma and had lost a lot of blood. His collarbone was sticking out from a huge wound in his neck. "They don't think he is going to make it," she said.

A flood of anxiety could have overtaken us, but I still felt an incredible peace. When my husband called the doctor, he informed, "David is in critical condition. Get here as soon as possible."

God did something miraculous for us that night. He gave us a gift of faith-filled prayer and all-encompassing peace, which helped us to believe Him over the reports we were hearing. We were thankful that our pastor had prayed for us before we left, and we knew many others were praying for our son. Then we prayed in faith, knowing that God loved David more than we did and that He knew what was best for him.

"You're a healing God!" my husband declared. We believed for a miracle.

When we arrived at the hospital at 2 a.m., we couldn't find the right building. Finally, a nurse escorted us to the trauma center. Another nurse greeted us and searched for a place where we could sit and discuss the facts and prognosis with the doctor. As we passed one room, we noticed a circle of doctors standing around a patient in a bed with light radiating from it. I peeked in, not knowing it was David. A nurse pulled the curtains shut.

Finally, we were escorted to the consultation room. The doctor started with the positives. David was moving his fingers, he didn't appear to have brain damage, and there was no internal bleeding.

I felt God had already answered our prayers. Everything would be okay. I asked, "So what's the problem?"

"He received a major blow to the heart, and we're concerned it will give out," the doctor explained. "We've given him three different heart medications, but he's not responding. His blood pressure is dangerously low, hovering around 59/24. He's not stable enough for exploratory procedures, so the next twenty-four hours will be critical."

When we walked into the ICU room, the consultants still circled my son's bed. As we moved to his bedside, the doctors' eyes fixed on us. Richie asked if we could pray.

"Lord, we trust you. You're a healing God. You've raised people from the dead, and now we're asking you to heal David. Our confidence is in you! We're asking for a miracle."

Since God's Word tells us to come boldly to the throne of grace, we did just that. We wanted God to shine through this situation. We decided that we wouldn't let the facts hinder our faith. And one by one we witnessed a series of miracles.

The next morning, David's blood pressure had stabilized enough so they could put in a balloon pump. I felt encouraged, though later I found out this procedure was considered a last resort. They told us the pump could stay in for up to seventy-two hours to enable David's heart to work on its own, but he only needed it for twenty-four hours!

Another small miracle. That night, the resident doctor gave us a positive report. My husband told him that many people were praying for David and for us. God's peace surrounded us like a warm blanket, though there were still more hurdles ahead.

Our once energetic and athletic boy now lay surrounded by tubes and monitors, pale and immobile. He had been in a drug-induced coma for three days and had only briefly opened his eyes to say hi. By Wednesday, he began to talk, though he didn't remember anything about the accident. It was the first time after the trauma that he ate any food—mashed potatoes. The following day he underwent extensive surgery on his neck and arm.

On the night of the accident, the gash near his collarbone was five inches wide and eight inches long! If paramedics who lived near the scene had not responded quickly, David would have bled to death. We were so thankful God had provided exactly what David needed, and we rejoiced. The surgery was successful.

A week after the accident, David was moved to a regular hospital room. I soon realized the staff there didn't know much about him. Though strict orders had been given for David to stay in a neck brace, the doctor on that floor ordered it off because David pulled at it. Then they wanted to insert a feeding tube, even after he had begun to eat on his own. My heart took a nose-dive when I saw how they mishandled situations and called him "unresponsive." I felt that all the gains David made would be lost if we didn't do something. Once again, we turned to God and the power of prayer.

After these events, we went back to the trauma ICU and explained that we weren't happy with his current care. The following day, they moved David into a step-down unit. I felt that God had, once again, answered our prayers. Many people had been alerted in our church and around the country and were still praying for him. By then, even the doctors had started calling him the miracle boy. They originally hadn't expected him to make it through the first night.

Though the facts appeared depressing from the start, God kept giving me hope and comfort. He surrounded me with His awesome peace even when the nurse gave us a disheartening report: David would need three months of rehabilitation and up to a year of around-the-clock in-house care. She read a litany of things David would no longer be able to do, such as feed or clothe himself. At first, I felt confused, but I continued to pray God's Word.

The resident doctor gave us a very different account. He said David should be back to normal within three to four weeks instead of months. My heart soared.

I remember when David was given permission to get out of his hospital bed and sit in a chair. I remember how excited he was. Instead of just sitting up, he hopped over the rail with his heart monitor and catheter trailing behind. He nearly knocked over all the machinery. It was an exasperating, yet exhilarating, sight.

Soon he was receiving a ton of visitors. David loved it and couldn't stop talking. He discussed in detail how to put together a complicated bicycle. Every day after that, he gained more and more intellectual and physical ability. God was miraculously answering our prayers, minute by minute.

On the day of David's release, all the doctors were happy to see their miracle boy walk out the door without a wheelchair. The same nurse who had given us the hopeless news early on, discharged him with tears in her eyes, saying, "I've never seen someone who needed an aortic balloon pump walk out of the hospital."

I didn't really understand the full extent of that miracle until we visited David's home, Block Island, a week after his release. People recounted the serious accident, all the blood he lost, and the thirty-second response of the neighbors who just happened to be paramedics. I knew it wasn't just coincidence. It was God's provision for David. Throughout this whole ordeal, God spoke to me over and over again about the power of faith, of believing His Word over the facts.

Eight years have passed since his accident, and David is doing well—no rehab for him for the rest of his life! He now has a son, a good job, and a winning smile. He's heard over and over again that he's a miracle boy, and I'm praying he'll realize just how much his life is a living, breathing testimony to God's healing power.

A Sparkling Miracle

GAIL R. HELGESON

May this be a trip that will awaken my desire to trust God more . . . to trust that He will keep us safe and teach me to thrive. Maybe it will open my eyes to see Him; I want more of Him.

Those words from my journal haunted me as we stood at the airport in Rome after a delayed flight from Paris. Hungry and worn, my husband and I had shuffled off the plane and followed the other passengers, herded together like a flock of sheep, to the baggage claim area. As the baggage carousel circled, black bags descended the chute and into the arms of the waiting travelers. So many bags looked alike I wondered how they didn't get lost.

Then I looked around and realized everyone had grabbed his or her bags and left. That is, everyone but us. Only after the carousel stopped did we realize our bags had taken an alternate vacation.

In the days leading to this vacation, I had spent much time in prayer and journaling. That's when I'd penned my paragraph about trusting God and wanting more of Him.

But now, on the first leg of our journey, I didn't expect the trust to have to start so soon.

There we stood, marooned in a foreign-to-us airport. We couldn't speak the language, and had no idea when, or if, we would see our bags again. The harsh glare of fluorescent lights stalked us as we hunted down the customer service counter.

The man behind the desk seemed to care more about the score on the TV screen than about our missing luggage. We couldn't do anything except fill out forms and let the airport officials know where we would be should our bags appear.

Frustrated, we left empty-handed through the airport doors. Soon we discovered luggage wasn't the only thing we would lose.

Travel can be exhausting. You have to be even more aware of your surroundings than normal. We read that taxi drivers may try to rip you off. We were determined not to let that happen as we flagged down a taxi and slid into the back seat.

With a cigarette drooping between his lips, the driver pushed the fare button. We rolled the windows down and gasped for air that wasn't smoke-laden as we took off. Horns blew, cars whizzed through red lights, and scooters buzzed around like mosquitoes.

We arrived safely at our hotel, passed the fee to the driver, and exited the vehicle. The irritated man waved the money at us and shouted, "No, no. No enough. You short me."

We apologized and handed over more euros. He smiled, gave us a thumbs-up, and helped us cross the busy street to our hotel. Only after we checked in, did we calculate and realize we'd been had.

With no luggage, and fifty euros poorer, we were crabby. We got to our room, and although we were tempted to sulk and stay in for the night, we realized Rome was out there. The Vatican walls stood directly across from our hotel window. Grateful that I had my journal tucked in my backpack, I opened it to the verses penned inside the front cover. One in particular jumped from the page—Psalm 31:14: "But I trust in you, Lord; I say, 'You are my God.'"

My husband and I prayed and asked for protection, and for God to give us glimpses of His presence. I wiped some tears, washed up as best I could, and off we went. We enjoyed our first bites of fresh Italian pizza and scrumptious gelato. Airplane food had sustained us, but this feast replenished our souls.

We wandered back to the hotel, and before I collapsed into bed, I removed my earrings and laid them on the desk. *I probably should not set them here*, I thought, but I did anyway.

My husband uses a CPAP machine to sleep, and, of course, it was in his AWOL suitcase. Between his snores and the adjustment of an unfamiliar place, we spent a restless night.

Thankful we packed some clothes in our carry-on bags, we prepared for the day ahead. Our first full day in Rome involved a tour of the Vatican. I reached for the earrings I had placed on the desk, baffled to find only one. Distressed, I looked all over. The earring was gone! I was devastated, and since my husband had fumbled around at the desk the night before, it was easy to play the blame game.

What made it worse was that these were my favorite pair of earrings—diamond teardrops I'd bought in England a few years earlier and wore everywhere.

Their sentimental value meant more than their monetary value. I'd dreamed of taking a trip to England since I'd been in the eighth grade, and had never imagined that day would come. My parents had known about my dream but died before it came to fruition. I finally did get to go years later, and those earrings were my keepsake; I often thought of my parents when I wore them. When I was packing for this trip, I'd thought about leaving the earrings at home since they meant so much to me. But I'd squelched the idea, thinking, *What could go wrong?*

I could taste the salt from the tears that rolled down my cheeks. Heat rose up my neck and anger clouded my judgment. Venom spewed from my mouth straight at my husband. "Why didn't you see my earrings on the desk? You lost my earring. The pair I adore most. It's all your fault."

"Me? You're the one who put them there. Why is it my fault?" he retorted.

In the twelve hours we had been in Rome, we had managed to lose our luggage, euros, sleep, patience, tempers, and now my favorite earring.

Dejected, my husband picked up his backpack and pulled out a flashlight. I'd kidded him about the flashlight when we were packing. I'd laughed and said, "What are you bringing that for? You don't need that."

"You never know when you will need one," he'd responded.

I recalled those words and hugged him. I said I was sorry and thanked him for his wisdom. We dropped to our knees and shined the light in the dark corners of our hotel room. We shook the curtains and inspected every piece of paper on the desk. We checked windowsills and overturned garbage. We made the bed three times and rubbed our bare feet across the tile floor. We found plenty of dust bunnies, but no earring. It had simply disappeared.

We needed to go; the Vatican awaited. But first, I wanted to get alone and pray. Outside our room, a deck beckoned. Small tables with fresh flowers filled the area and none were occupied. I settled into a cushioned seat and pondered the fact that losing the earring was my fault, too. I should not have loosely placed them on the desk. Perhaps those earrings were a possession I held too tightly to, or maybe they were tied too closely to the memory of my parents, who supported my dream. Either way, I had to learn that I could trust only in God. I prayed and asked God to somehow help us find that earring, and if not, to help me to let it go. I couldn't ignore the irony of being in a part of the world where the faithful journey on pilgrimages, while I was undergoing my own trust journey.

We visited the Vatican, and learned how Michelangelo painted the most famous ceiling in the world, and then we toured other famous sites. But at the end of the day, we still didn't have our luggage, and the earring was still lost.

We woke the third day to find my husband's luggage outside our door. Opening his suitcase was a bit like opening a gift on Christmas morning. There were toiletries, his sleep machine, and some of my clothes, since friends had advised us to load clothes in each other's bags "just in case your luggage gets lost."

Time was running out. The next day we would leave Rome— possibly without my luggage and, even more likely, without my earring. Once again I whispered a prayer, asking God to specifically supply my earring.

That afternoon, I sat in a pew in a cathedral, staring at a statue of Jesus bearing His cross. In the quietness, God had my full attention. Did I have enough faith to trust Him with my whole life, even a lost earring? Finally, I had to let go. *Okay, God. You win. You get control. Help my unbelief.*

We awoke our last day in Rome without my luggage. We peacefully walked downstairs and enjoyed a fresh breakfast. When we were about to enter the elevator to return to our room, the gal at the front desk stopped us. She spoke with such excitement, I had to ask her to repeat herself. "Your luggage here!"

"Really? Are you serious? It's here?"

She wheeled the familiar black bag with the pink bandana from behind the desk. I was in awe, but God wasn't done yet.

After I enjoyed a shower using my own items, I changed and zipped up the suitcase. We closed the hotel door and rolled our bags to the elevator. I decided to leave my address with the front desk just in case my earring was found. I gave it to the same woman who delivered my luggage.

"We do find thing sometimes and put in this drawer," the woman said in her broken English. She opened a cabinet under the desk. "I remember housekeeping telling me something like you say was found while empty vacuum. She say she almost dump, but she notice sparkle. Not sure it yours, but let us look."

She dangled my diamond earring between her fingertips. I trembled as I scurried behind the desk to hug her.

"You have no idea what this means to me!" I exclaimed.

"I think I do," she replied.

I wept. I looked toward my husband who, through his own tears, replied, "We are blessed. This is a miracle."

I had never seen a housekeeper at the hotel. Only once could we tell someone had come in and cleaned. The fact that she had noticed a flicker through the dust and dirt in that vacuum bag speaks of God's hand. She could have thrown the contents into the garbage. Perhaps she could have kept the earring for herself. Who would know? Instead, she gave it to the front desk.

Angels come in many forms. In my case, the angel was a housekeeper. That earring was nowhere to be found. We looked everywhere. There is no other explanation as to why I wear it today. Ephesians 3:20–21 states, "Now to him who is able to do immeasurably more than all we ask or imagine, according to his power that is at work within us, to him be the glory . . . for ever and ever." And Luke 15:8–9 tells the story of a woman who loses a coin and rejoices when she finds it.

I, too, have rejoiced since my earring was recovered. True, it is a small miracle. But it is a constant reminder, whenever I wear my earrings, of His longing to give me the desires of my heart. My job is to simply trust Him.

A Precise Prayer for Healing

SUSAN L. TUTTLE

Your mother has cancer."

I gripped the phone as I listened to Dad's choked-up voice. In my thirty-four years, I'd heard that word more times in relation to my mother than a daughter ever should.

I sucked in a breath. I didn't want to go on this ride again, but cancer offers no choice. It tosses you to the front of the line and thrusts you onto its crazy roller coaster without asking permission.

Silence hung between us. Dad always had positive words to say. Encouragement to give. But not this time. It was so unlike the other times he'd delivered this news.

I sucked in a fortifying breath, resolving to once again believe and speak the words Dad couldn't. Those words he'd used with each previous diagnosis that now seemed stuck in his throat. "We'll beat this."

And we would. I didn't want to consider any other option. "It doesn't look good." Tears filled his voice. It was the first time I'd heard my father cry over my mother's health.

My stomach tightened. With my free hand I massaged my temples as I lowered myself onto my bed.

"What did the doctor say, Dad?" I wasn't sure I wanted to know.

He cleared his throat and took a moment. "We've been to several, and they're all saying the same thing." Again he faltered. "They're telling her to go home and enjoy the time she has left. Six months, a year tops. There's nothing they can do."

A lump lodged in my throat. Six months? She'd never been given a time allotment before. The calendar flipped through my mind, time slipping away. How do you plan your last Thanksgiving, your last Christmas—your last anything with someone you love?

"How's Mom?"

With a shaky voice he answered, "She says this might be the one she doesn't beat."

Cancer hadn't come only to do battle this time. It had come to war and win.

We regrouped as a family. Reading over her diagnosis in black and white, things looked dark. A tumor was growing in close proximity to her pancreas. They'd tested the cells. Pancreatic cancer. The five-year survival rate fell under 5 percent, but they reiterated that due to the intricacies of her case, they couldn't even guarantee a year.

With the tumor encased around a major vein, no one wanted to touch what promised to be an impossible surgery. At best, it would extend her life by a few months. Worst-case scenario: She could bleed out on the table.

All doctors in our area refused her case—which spoke volumes. We lived in the suburbs of Grand Rapids, Michigan, known as the Medical Mile, aptly named for the millions of research dollars that had been poured into our city. Schools had added campuses simply to be close to the medical advances in the heart of our downtown.

If no one there was willing to help her, who would be?

We prayed desperately for wisdom, and God led my parents to a doctor nearly three hours away on the east side of the state. My parents met with a surgeon who agreed to evaluate her case. We gathered as a family shortly afterward.

"So?" My older brother voiced the question we all wondered.

Mom, perched on the dark wooden chair at the worn kitchen table where we'd grown up eating, folded her hands over her stomach.

"The surgeon took my case before the tumor board. They agreed I at least deserve a chance." For the first time since this started, she smiled. "They're going to do the surgery."

We clung to that hope, and it bolstered our spirits even if we knew the tumor board was humoring us. They didn't truly believe the surgery would be successful. With the tumor measuring eight centimeters and its precarious location, this surgery was more about allowing us to let her go, knowing we'd tried everything we could before uttering our good-byes. It was their way of offering hope.

But the hope we felt wasn't from the doctors.

Our hope came from the Lord.

With a new plan facing us, we bathed the day of surgery in prayer, our church congregation, extended family, and friends joining us. Hope continued to rise even in the midst of an impossible situation.

The night before the procedure, as I packed at my own home, my parents received a call from our pastor.

"I've been praying for you, and God has placed on my heart something specific to share. I wonder if I can come over."

"Definitely," Dad answered. Prayer was the most important action we knew we could take, and we'd absorb all the prayers we could.

Pastor Sam arrived at their house, and the three of them huddled in the family room. Mom settled into the red recliner she'd purchased for my father, but which had quickly become her favorite chair. In the comfort and quiet of their own home, our pastor anointed her with oil and prayed for her healing. In that prayer, he declared five specific things:

The tumor would be completely encapsulated.

The tumor would separate from the main vein without the need to cut.

The tumor would fall out into the surgeon's hands.

There would be clear margins on the tumor.

And regardless of what the pathology report currently said, when they tested the tumor after removing it, there would be no evidence of pancreatic cancer at all.

After praying these things, Pastor Sam left.

The next day, my entire family caravanned across the state to the Karmanos Cancer Institute. On March 11, 2008, we hugged Mom good-bye as they wheeled her into the operating room. We then settled in the large waiting room with so many others who longed to see their loved ones healed.

The chair crinkled as I sat, hard beneath my weight. How unreal. Had I just said good-bye to my mother? Yes, my hope came from the Lord, but it was feeling battered. With every cancer diagnosis, I wondered if it was the last one she'd receive—and this time the foe was so formidable. Could I trust Him again? I struggled to hold tight to the truth I knew: God is the greatest physician of all.

And He was the one who operated on her right now.

Throughout the morning, friends and other family members showed up to comfort us, sharing stories that made us laugh or simply waiting with us in silence. Unsure of how long we would wait for the surgeon and his report, this outpouring of love helped us pass the time.

Several long hours ticked by before a nurse came into the waiting room. She approached Dad. "We'd like to have you all come back to a room so the surgeon can speak with you."

Wide-eyed, my sister and I gaped at the woman. There was only one reason I'd ever heard of them delivering news in seclusion.

"What if we don't want to go back to that room?" I asked.

She smiled. "You do. It's good. I promise."

The bands of anxiety squeezing my chest released.

She led all of us to a tiny gray room with a small wooden table and chairs. Some of us sat while others leaned against the wall. As awkward silence descended, we began to recount more funny stories about Mom. In the midst of our nervous laughter, the surgeon entered the room, his blue scrubs showing a few faint lines of sweat while his hair remained hidden under his cap and a white surgical mask hung around his neck.

He crossed his arms, slightly shaking his head. His eyes focused downward before scanning each of us.

"I don't know what you're doing, but whatever it is, keep doing it." Then he stared Dad in the eye. "That tumor was completely contained. It wasn't involved with the vein. I didn't even have to cut"—again he shook his head—"I don't know why, but it just fell out into my hand. All margins were clean." He paused. "We'll have to wait a few weeks for pathology reports, but it appeared to be nothing more than a cyst. Not at all what we saw on the reports."

This surgeon unknowingly had just repeated nearly verbatim the words our pastor had prayed over Mom.

Dad smiled. "We know why."

It was the second time I'd ever seen him cry over my mother's health, and this time they were tears of joy.

Six weeks later, Mom and Dad sat in the oncologist's office as she repeated the final item our pastor had been led to pray.

"Your pathology report is clean. There's not one pancreatic cancer cell in that tumor." She lifted her shoulders, in awe of what she saw on the medical report. "Other than healing from the surgery, there's nothing else to do."

The medical community was amazed at Mom's case and left without explanation, but my parents offered it to them anyway. God instructed our pastor to pray over her. He was obedient and delivered the words he'd been given, praying specifically how the Holy Spirit led him. Yet our pastor's words didn't heal her; he was simply a messenger. The surgeon didn't heal her either; he was simply an instrument.

The Great Physician alone deserved all of the credit. Not only did He sew together my battered hope and remind me that in all situations I could trust Him, but He ultimately did what no one else would or could do. He healed my mom. Once again. Miraculously.

About the Contributors

Jeff Adams is an award-winning author and pastor. He lives in Arizona with his wife and daughter. He teaches what he's learned, and he learns so that he may teach.

Jan Apilado is an author and chaplain, along with her husband, for three different military organizations. They are retired pastors living in the Oregon Cascade mountains.

James Stuart Bell is a publishing veteran and compiler of this volume and approximately forty other volumes of short stories. He has cover credit on more than one hundred books and owns Whitestone Communications.

Holly Blevins is a wife and mom living in Berryville, Virginia, where she's a youth leader at BLAZE ministries. She loves leading worship, hiking, and writing.

Laura L. Bradford is an award-winning poet and author. Her works have appeared in CHICKEN SOUP and GUIDEPOSTS books, as well as other compilations.

AnnaLee Conti, ordained minister and teacher, resides in the Mid-Hudson Valley, New York, with her pastor husband, Bob. She has published books, short stories, and articles.

Jenni Davenport is a Midwest mom who works as an editor during the day, is a freelancer at night, and has a circus of kids in her house every weekend.

Betty Johnson Dalrymple is a contributor to numerous devotional books, such as *God Allows U-Turns*, *Chicken Soup for the Soul*, and *Love Is a Verb*. She facilitates a grief support group.

Brenda Dillon has a horse farm in Michigan and would rather be in the barn than in the kitchen. Her love for Jesus is the pivot point in her life.

Beth Duewel is a mother of three, trying to hit the mark with her mom's meatloaf recipe for Jerry. The paper angel still tops the Christmas tree. Coming in 2017: *Fix-Her-Upper: Hope and Laughter Through a God Renovated Life!* by Beth Duewel and Rhonda Rhea.

Anita Estes resides in the Hudson Valley with her husband and various pets. She is in *Who's Who of American Teachers*. She is the author of *When God Speaks* and *Letters to God on a Prodigal Son*.

Virginia Rose Fairbrother has been a pastor's wife, ESL teacher, and writer. She and David have been married forty-six years. They have three children and six grandchildren.

Ellen Farrington's works are published online and in several books and magazines. She holds advanced degrees in the biological sciences and lives with her family in New England.

Anna M. Gregory and her husband are blessed with five sons and numerous grandchildren. She writes devotionals as God gives her the words to encourage others.

Dorothy J. Haire is a retired speech-language pathologist and a retired pastor who has earned four degrees. She is writing a commentary on the book of James.

Charles Earl Harrel served as a pastor for thirty years. He has more than 350 published works.

Cassie Harris is an aspiring author who loves to watch God at work. She is attending Grace College and pursuing a degree in journalism and biblical studies.

Gail R. Helgeson continues to daily put her trust in God. She finds joy in writing, travel, and spending time with her husband and two grown children.

Charles J. Huff lives in Aurora, Illinois, with his wife of forty-plus years. He has been published at christiandevotions.us. Find his blog at chashuff.wordpress.com.

LaRose Karr enjoys speaking and ministering to God's people. Her family is her greatest blessing. She believes her writing is a gift from God and gives Him all the glory!

Donna Lee (Shane) Loomis is a wife of fifty years, mother, and grandmother. Family, children, writing, and sharing God's love are her greatest passions.

Joyce Starr Macias is a freelance writer and a retired newspaper reporter. She specializes in stories about her personal walk with God that have appeared in several magazines and books.

Marleen McDowell and her family pioneer in their solar home deep in the Cascade mountains. Marleen enjoys the forest animals, gardening, canning, sewing, and sharing Jesus through her writings.

Marybeth Mitcham is an emerging freelance author whose writings have been published online and in the *Christmas Moments #2* anthology.

Susan Allen Panzica is a speaker, Bible teacher, writer of the Eternity Cafe blog, and executive director of Justice Network, which raises awareness about human trafficking.

Marty Prudhomme is a freelance writer who has written and taught Bible studies for twenty years. She serves as Louisiana vice president of Leaders Training for Aglow International.

Janice Richardson writes Christian articles and stories focusing on how God is impacting people's lives. She resides in Calgary, Alberta, with her husband and the youngest of three sons.

Bobbie Roper is a retired pastor's wife and mother of four and has ten grandchildren. She is a women's Bible study teacher, seminar leader, and freelance writer.

Bill Shane (October 11, 1923—March 12, 2003) was a Colorado native. Bill devoted his life, from the age of eight, to God, family, and friends. A self-taught man, he was ingenious, inventive, hardworking, trustworthy, charitable, and creative.

A loving, caring family man who believed God had a special purpose for his family and supported that in the way he lived his life.

David Michael Smith is a writer of inspirational short stories, a church deacon, a faithful husband, and a loving father from Georgetown, Delaware. Email him at davidandgeri@hotmail.com.

Evelyn Rhodes Smith and her husband, Ted, live in Edgewood Summit, a retirement community in Charleston, West Virginia. Her stories appear in A Cup of Comfort series and volumes for Bethany House Publishers.

Ray Stenner was forced to retire due to illness, but keeps busy with renovations and volunteer work with his loving wife, Rose, and enjoys time with their family.

Delores E. Topliff lives near Minneapolis. She loves Jesus, family, grandchildren, friends, writing, college teaching, mission trips, travel, and her small farm.

Faith Turnet is a North Carolina veteran educator and enjoys travel. She speaks to churches through her Devoted Diva Ministry.

Susan L. Tuttle lives in Michigan, where she's happily married to her best friend, is a home-schooling mom of three, and loves to write encouraging stories.

Elfriede Volk has been married for fifty-three years and has four children and eight grandchildren. She and her husband work as volunteer missionaries in various parts of the world.

Susan M. Watkins is featured in multiple publications and on CBN.com. Additional credits include Gloria Gaynor's *We Will Survive* and Max Lucado's *HisIsMine.com*.

Melinda Wright (as told to **Anita Estes**) is the wife of a church planter, mother of three, and grandmother of four. She loves cooking, hiking, entertaining, camping, and watching how God brings forth life.

Dr. Joshua F. Younce is a chiropractic physician in the western suburbs of Chicago. He served as team doctor for Wheaton Academy. Josh is married to Cheri, with two children, Sydney and Jackson.

James Stuart Bell is a Christian publishing veteran and the owner of Whitestone Communications, a literary development agency. He is the editor of many story collections, including *Angels, Miracles, and Heavenly Encounters*; *Heaven Touching Earth*; and *Encountering Jesus*, as well as the coauthor of numerous books in the COMPLETE IDIOT'S GUIDE series. He has cover credit on more than one hundred books, and he and his wife live in a western suburb of Chicago.

More True Stories of God's Love and Provision

Compiled by James Stuart Bell

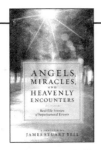

This fascinating look at the supernatural world offers more than forty true stories of miraculous provision, encounters with angels and demons, near-death experiences, and incredible rescues. You'll marvel at how God and His angels are working behind the scenes to protect and guide us.

Angels, Miracles, and Heavenly Encounters

Miracles, healing, divine provision and protection— this compilation of true, uplifting stories will touch your heart, strengthen your faith, and remind you that, even when it seems God isn't at work in your life, there is a loving Father who is always working on your behalf.

Heaven Touching Earth

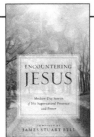

In this inspiring collection, people who have seen Jesus, heard His voice, or experienced His miraculous intervention share their amazing stories. You'll find hope and encouragement in these accounts of Jesus' ongoing intervention in the lives of believers like you.

Encountering Jesus